House Beautiful

1000 SENSATIONAL MAKEOVERS

House Beautiful
1000 SENSATIONAL MAKEOVERS

From the Editors of *House Beautiful*

HEARST BOOKS
New York

HEARST BOOKS
New York

An Imprint of Sterling Publishing
387 Park Avenue South
New York, NY 10016

This book was previously published as two hardcovers under the titles *500 Sensational Ways to Create Your Ideal Home* and *500 Makeovers: Great Ideas & Quick Changes*.

Library of Congress Cataloging-in-Publication Data available upon request.

2 4 6 8 10 9 7 5 3 1

www.housebeautiful.com

For information about custom editions, special sales, premium and corporate purchases, please contact Sterling Special Sales Department at 800-805-5489 or specialsales@sterlingpublishing.com.

Distributed in Canada by Sterling Publishing
c/o Canadian Manda Group, 165 Dufferin Street
Toronto, Ontario, Canada M6K 3H6

Distributed in Australia by Capricorn Link (Australia) Pty. Ltd.
P.O. Box 704, Windsor, NSW 2756 Australia

Manufactured in China

Sterling ISBN 978-1-58816-889-4

WOLF

Contents

Introduction 8
Chapter 1 Balance 12
Chapter 2 Simplicity 72
Chapter 3 Impact 138
Chapter 4 Function 218
Chapter 5 Details 298
Chapter 6 Color 356
Chapter 7 Quick Fixes 432
Chapter 8 Sophisticated Surroundings 490
Chapter 9 Eclectic Environment 572
Chapter 10 Serene Retreat 632
Chapter 11 Comfortable Haven 692
Chapter 12 Natural Abode 748
Chapter 13 Bold Domain 806
Chapter 14 The Welcoming Home 870
Photo Credits 948
Index 954

Introduction

A HOME SHOULD DO MORE than provide shelter and creature comforts. It should also enhance your daily routine, brighten your spirits, stimulate your imagination, and ignite your passions. In short, the perfect home should reflect both who you are and who you want to become. Designing a home, like cultivating a life, should be embraced as a pleasurable work in progress—the process is usually full of surprises, and it never happens overnight. The best homes evolve over time, just as people do.

The lure of a "makeover" is hard to resist: Everyone loves to see a room reinvented into a new and beautiful setting. But remember that making over a room doesn't have to be about changing it completely. Nor does it require an expert dictating the terms of the redo. Instead of assuming you will need to start from scratch, think of a makeover as starting fresh. Approached in this way, you'll be in charge of what to tweak, change, or replace—and you can create an environment that reinforces your values and how you want to live. When you cultivate spaces that support your core needs, values, and ideals, you won't wind up with cookie-cutter rooms or spaces that look like those of your next-door neighbor. Nor will your décor be driven by tradition or trends. Instead, your home will be an extension of your personality and your dreams.

Whether you plan to work with a designer or tackle your decorating challenges on your own, the ideas on the pages that follow can fuel the process and offer inspiration along the way. Each chapter breaks down the often-daunting prospect of redoing an entire room into smaller, more manageable tasks. The hundreds of accompanying photographs of beautiful spaces will also inspire you to create the rooms of your dreams.

The first half of *1000 Sensational Makeovers* is organized by six basic design elements: Balance, Simplicity, Impact, Function, Details, and Color. Applied to the primary components that define a roomthese essential elements provide a firm foundation for any makeover project, large or small.

The second half of this book hones in on the home of your dreams. In chapters 8 through 14, you'll find seven different lifestyle ideals—or dreams, if you will: Sophisticated Surroundings, Eclectic Environment, Serene Retreat, Comfortable Haven, Natural Abode, Bold Domain, and the Welcoming Home. They were developed with an emphasis on personality types and inner needs, rather than style, to help you clarify what is most important to you as you cultivate the highest quality of life you can imagine.

The rooms in one chapter may resonate with you immediately, while spaces in another might appeal to your spouse. More likely you'll see spaces and ideas in two or three chapters that support complementary or even conflicting lifestyles. The key is to look for the dominant themes that rise to the top and balance the dreams of everyone who shares your home.

Whatever the scope of your project—cozy room or expansive space, minor update or major overhaul—these ideas, tips, and tricks will help you clarify your vision and realize that change is easy, refreshing, and invigorating.

GRILLING
THE WAY TO COOK
WORLD ATLAS
ENCARTA DICTIONARY

Chapter 1 Balance

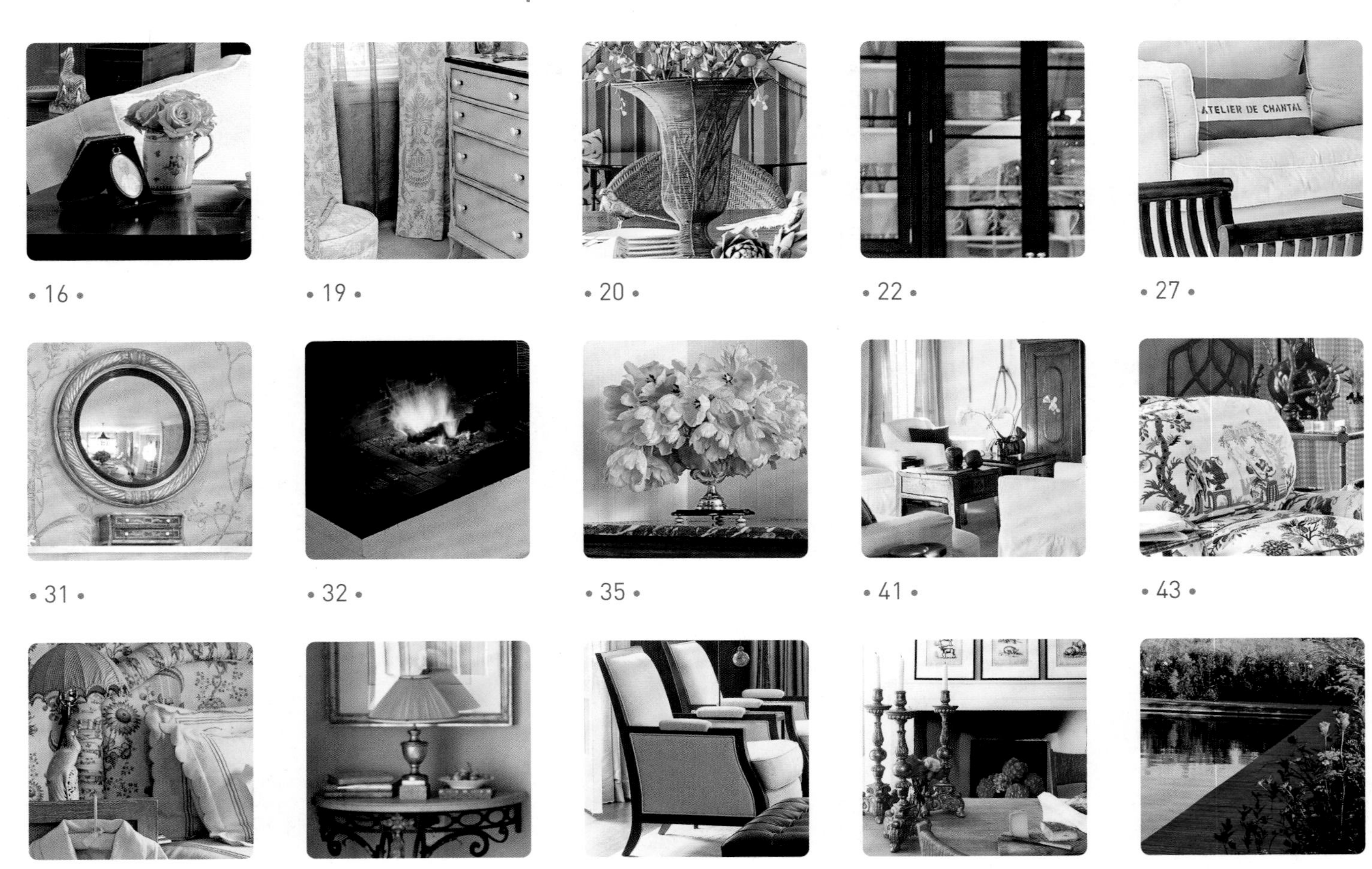

• 16 • • 19 • • 20 • • 22 • • 27 •
• 31 • • 32 • • 35 • • 41 • • 43 •
• 46 • • 53 • • 54 • • 58 • • 70 •

IT ISN'T NECESSARY to understand the principles of classical design to appreciate the value of balance in a room. When you walk into a well-proportioned space, you'll know it—and you'll feel instinctively at ease. Symmetry (identical sconces flanking a mantel, a fixture whose size perfectly complements the table it hangs above) plays a part. But balance is also about improbable pairings: light and dark, old and new, casual and formal, masculine and feminine, large and small, hard and soft. You might not think, for example, to match a bold geometric print with a buttoned-up settee, or a radiant crystal chandelier with a rustic painted cabinet. Yet these sorts of juxtapositions keep a room from feeling one-note. Indeed, they work in concert to create a glorious harmony.

1

•

Paneling that extends halfway to the ceiling—here in a two-story living room—makes a grand space feel more cozy. The beige walls above add depth and warmth.

2

A band of ornate crown molding can make a formal space even more luxurious. In this room, the floral details in the molding are picked up in the carpet and the curtains in the adjoining room.

3

A tall, antique mirror—carefully arranged to be almost level with the tops of the doorframes and the crown molding—suits this room's lofty scale.

4

Painted paneling and a unique railing (here made to resemble tree branches) bring texture to a stairwell. In this room, the symmetrical display of engravings and chromolithographs is equally eye-catching from a high or low vantage point.

5

Establish a sense of harmony in a small space by limiting the palette to one color. The walls in this beige sitting room are covered with a pale yellow hand-painted damask wallpaper, which provides the perfect backdrop for a collection of like-colored antique furnishings.

6

Nature-inspired accents—here stenciled leaf motifs on a pair of built-in china cabinets and a collection of framed fish prints—enliven and bring subtle color to a white-walled dining room.

7

Rich, wooden floor-to-ceiling china cabinets—inspired by library shelves—are at home in a dining room with generous proportions. Outfitted with sliding glass doors and a rolling ladder, the cupboards allow for an impressive display.

8

Intricately patterned floor tiles painted in shades of cream, blue, and gray literally lay the groundwork for the color scheme in this sleek, modern kitchen. Varied textures—stone, metal, wood, tufted suede—enrich the cool palette.

9

Chocolate brown wood floors ground an airy kitchen and provide a lively contrast when matched with pale, gray-green cabinets and light gray honed and waxed granite countertops.

10

A pale blue-and-cream checkerboard pattern painted on a wood floor becomes even more charming with age and wear. Here, a grid of overhead bleached beams reinforces the geometric design.

11

Keep a contemporary kitchen from feeling too cold by incorporating a few whimsical elements. Here, a rough-hewn wooden island painted cherry red and a bright blue oven door are juxtaposed against ebony-stained cabinets and a stainless-steel backsplash.

12

Large terra-cotta floor tiles give a breezy, Mediterranean villa–feel to a room. Here, they serve as a lovely foil for an elegant marble tub and other clean white furnishings.

13

Go the unexpected route. In this sunroom, instead of installing French doors, the owners opted for custom-designed stable doors made from Douglas fir. The wood doors also harmonize with the structure's ceiling beams and the modern furnishings.

A BUILDING IS NOT 4 WALLS
BUT RATHER THE SPACE CONTAINED
WITHIN THOSE WALLS.
ATELIER DE CHANTAL

14

Shake up styles: A mod print on a traditional English settee looks fresh; matching contemporary armchairs with plaid throw pillows have a similar effect.

15

For a serene, unfussy look in a casual space, think in pairs—here, twin alabaster lamps, matching chairs upholstered in nubby pale blue fabric, dark-wood side tables—and stick to two dominant colors.

16

While a pair of vintage stools covered in chocolate-colored leather might blend into one setting, they gain presence amidst luminous white silk upholstery. The brown hue is picked up on tables scattered throughout the room.

17

Set up separate seating areas to help break up a large living room. Here, a graceful sofa and a pair of chairs flank the fireplace, while a fabric-draped table surrounded by upholstered benches provides a spot for books and magazines.

18

Hints of bright red pop against a backdrop of neutral furnishings in solids and patterns. Consider using the hue on throw pillows and seat cushions, and in surprising ways, such as peaking out from behind a set of curtains.

19

•

When a living room is dominated by one feature—here, a large, open fireplace—choose furniture that balances the scale of that feature, such as this oversized sofa.

20

This great room may be done in all neutrals, but it's anything but plain. Consider upholstering matching sofas in several subtly different fabrics. Here, the sofas feature gold fabric for the body, a pear shade for the seat cushions, and olive for the back cushions.

21

For a dramatic effect, look for a chandelier with a diameter that is approximately equal to that of the table it hangs above. The sinuous shape and rough, bleached finish on this fixture—found at a flea market—give it an elegant yet natural feel.

22

It's never dull to combine pieces made of the same materials—here, warm, ruddy wood—so long as each item has a distinct personality. In this foyer, an antique carved mirror, ornate console table, and English wheelback chairs all hold their own.

23

Expand the dimensions of a space by incorporating mirrors in unexpected ways. In this entry, an embellished antique oval piece is placed above a marble-topped console table with a square mirror mounted underneath.

24

●

It may seem counterintuitive to pair modern linen-upholstered chairs with a heavy antique mahogany dining table, but here it works beautifully. Note how the gray of the chairs is picked up in the mural and the rich tone of the wood is repeated on the sideboard. ◄◄

25

●

A stately antique elm trestle table and warm leather-upholstered chairs anchor this sunny kitchen. ◄

26

●

Sumptuous tufted suede chairs and a crystal chandelier look luxurious when set against a spare fireplace, simple antique hutch, and tile floors in a breakfast nook.

GRILLING
THE WAY TO COOK
WORLD ATLAS
ENCARTA DICTIONARY

27

Masculine (glossy black shelves, bull-fighting imagery) meets feminine (floral-print wrap-around sofa) in this cozy den. The lattice style of the shelves keeps them from seeming heavy.

28

Create a glamorous, ethereal look in a guest bedroom to promote comfort and relaxation—achieved here with a champagne-colored chaise, glass baluster tables that practically disappear, and diaphanous curtains.

MUSTIQUE
ALBERTO PINTO

29

•

Using one dominant color and pattern enables you to mix styles with ease. Here, traditional plaid upholstery mingles effortlessly with a mod concentric square rug. The geometric theme is echoed in the light fixture and the boxy silhouettes of the dining chairs.

30

•

For a contemporary look, consider hanging the curtains for two windows (situated along the same wall) from a single rod. Generous fabric panels mounted several inches above the window frames create a sense of drama.

31

•

Make a cozy room feel more spacious by mounting large-scale wall hangings just below ceiling height. Here, a pair of coordinating Asian silk hangings—flanking a bleached oak entertainment unit—draws the eye upward.

32

When combining multiple patterns, think in terms of scale. In this colorful living room, a splashy floral print on the upholstery, medium-size lattice pattern on the carpet, and tiny checks on the curtains and pillows work in harmony.

33

Another way to connect otherwise incongruous patterns is with trim. Here, red piping and grosgrain ribbon accent the cushions and skirts (respectively) on the upholstered pieces, while thick scarlet fringe surrounds the pillows.

34

Unify a diverse collection of furnishings—here an elegant English recamier and four styles of chairs—with a single upholstery pattern. Ties connecting fabric and cushions to frames lend a pretty, feminine touch.

35

Regal gold curtains provide a warm counterpoint to bare floors and a cool pattern. Two rows of braid finished with fringe on the box-pleated valances echo the small embellishments on the slipcovers.

36

Upholstered dining chairs make an ornate breakfast nook feel cozy. In this room, the soft, sandy hues of the fabric, floor, and zinc chandelier, sparked in places by bits of gold, create a serene environment.

37

•

Give a motif an almost three-dimensional effect by layering matching patterns, as seen here on the walls, upholstered headboard, bed skirt, and curtain swag in a child's room. The bed seems less obtrusive when blended in with its surroundings—ideal in a tight space.

38

•

Patterned fabrics are typically used for bedclothes, but try them on a headboard and dust ruffle for a cozy look. Matching curtains help tie this room together, while a quilted coverlet and solid-colored chair and ottoman add texture.

39

Frame a bed or other beautiful piece of furniture by arranging it between two windows, each dressed with a single curtain panel (instead of the familiar pair) swept to one side. ◄◄

40

If there's a pattern you absolutely love, go all out with it. Here, a toile Roman shade and duvet cover—defined with a wide black trim—extend the wallpaper pattern in a cozy guest bedroom. Buffalo check fabric on the chairs provides graphic contrast. ◄

41

Curtains aren't just for windows. Suspended from a track mounted around the perimeter of the ceiling, they can also envelop a room with texture and softness.

42

Ensure a monochromatic room is never monotonous by choosing pieces in a range of materials—in this case stone, wood, and mirror, along with plush shag carpeting.

43

Avoid hanging pictures too high, which can look awkward and force viewers to crane their necks. The center of this antique Italian fresco is at eye level and doesn't quite clear the pillows on the bench below—a casual touch in a formal entryway.

44

Let a room's dominant design elements, such as architecture or wallpaper, dictate how you decorate. In this foyer, ladder-like étagères mimic the pattern of the windows around the front door.

45

A colorful, crisply pleated tablecloth in a dramatic floral print brightens a table in a foyer. Topped with a sheet of 1/4-inch-thick glass, cut to fit, the fabric topper serves as a lovely base for seasonal floral displays.

A WORLD HISTORY OF ART
Leonardo da Vinci
THE COMPLETE COLLECTION OF

46

In a pale, neutral room, a handful of dark pieces—such as flea-market prints in black-and-gold frames and bamboo chairs painted a shiny ebony hue—provide focal points.

47

Complement symmetrical aspects of a room—here, a door located in the center of a wall—by mirroring arrangements. In this room, two pairs of antique lithographs and two iron console tables, both topped with gleaming gold lamps, are identically arranged on each side of the door.

48

A pair of ornately patterned lighting fixtures brings a touch of old-world glamour to a room dominated by clean lines and modern shapes. In this room, the abstract pattern on the rug echoes the design of the cables used to suspend the lamps.

49

•

Let a magnificent view—here of a sweeping lawn and the ocean in the distance—take center stage by installing window treatments that won't compete for attention; neutral colors work best.

50

•

Create an intriguing mantel display by mixing elaborate pieces—intricately carved pagodas, a lavish gold frame—with more humble ones. These simple, basket-weave bud vases are filled with cheerful red ranunculus.

51

•

Towering arrangements of flowering branches (which here reiterate the motif on the wall), window treatments that hang to the floor, and a set of mirrors help make a small space appear roomier.

52

•

Not all artwork has to be hung. A series of prints propped up on a mantel feels modern and refreshingly informal. Bright hydrangeas set in the fireplace below offset the black-and-white scheme.

53

•

Ornate antique candlesticks bring a Baroque twist to a simple dining table. Arranging a few collectibles at one end of the table, instead of a pair in the center, looks less expected and won't block diners' views.

54

•

Small pictures have greater impact when displayed en masse. These eighteenth-century watercolors are arranged in tight rows—just like the beams overhead. The works fill a whole wall, to stunning effect.

55

This large, eat-in nook has two shades on each window—the lower can be closed for privacy while the upper remains open, allowing some natural light into the room. Or they can both be closed for complete privacy.

56

Mix and match different styles and eras for an eclectic table setting. Here, a new patterned teacup mingles gracefully with a vintage salad plate, Danish stoneware dinner plate, and chopstick-like utensils that were found at a flea market.

57

A few colorful dishes invigorate a collection of white china and make for an eye-catching, whimsical display when arranged inside window cabinets or on open shelving.

58

Bring outdoor-style lighting indoors. Here, unfussy metal Colonial lanterns look right at home in a classic, wood-paneled kitchen. Twice the size of traditional lanterns, the fixtures complement the spacious interior.

59

•

Bathroom walls inlaid with mirrors create a dazzling effect when the lights are on. In this room, the white-painted cabinetry, gleaming floor, and shiny metal of the lamps enhance the brightness.

60

•

A mostly white color scheme, metal side table, and sleek cabinet hardware lend a modern edge to a bathroom with rustic architecture. ▶

61

•

Consider how the aspects of a bathroom work together. Here, a freestanding vessel sink harmonizes with the luxurious soaking tub. ▶

62

Natural materials and accents look, well, natural on a sunporch. Stone, wicker, distressed wood, and plants atop antique pedestals define this sunny space.

63

Create a dramatic entry into a pool—here, a lush archway—by framing the steps with potted greenery such as small palm trees in giant urns. In this scenario, large planters also anchor the pool's opposite corners.

64

Break up a sweeping, sloped landscape—and make it easier to navigate—with sets of stone steps. These can be as artful as this semicircular design or as simple as the linear ledges beyond.

65

A formal garden is more engaging when you mix materials (weathered wood, stone) and shapes (rectangular, oval, and circular hedges, triangular obelisks). Here, the steps leading to a trellis-backed platform are reminiscent of an open-air theater.

66

A pool blends in with the landscape when surrounded by a simple wood deck and tall meadow plants such as goldenrod and orchard grasses.

67

A textural border of mixed grasses, shrubs, and plants with variegated leaves helps define a broad lawn. Choose flowers that bloom at different times throughout the year.

Chapter 2 Simplicity

• 77 • • 80 • • 84 • • 91 • • 93 •

• 97 • • 103 • • 107 • • 110 • • 117 •

• 120 • • 124 • • 129 • • 133 • • 137 •

TAKE A HARD LOOK at the rooms in your home. Do the majority of pieces in them bring you joy? If not, it's time to consider how you might pare down or rearrange the space. This isn't about turning every interior into a sterile, minimalist shrine; instead, think of it as creating an environment where the things you love can shine. It can be very freeing, for example, to remove the curtains from a window, taking full advantage of a spectacular view, or to pull up a busy area rug and discover how much more beautiful the carved legs of a sofa look against the bare floor. Also give some thought to the weight of your pieces. Floating shelves, a china cabinet filled with clear glassware, and Lucite chairs are all functional without feeling heavy or overwhelming. By designing a space where your items have room to breathe, you too will breathe easier.

68

Put the spotlight on an elegant staircase by choosing a creamy paint, a pale limestone floor, and a judicious mix of furnishings (note the almost completely bare walls and unadorned window in this entryway).

69

Give walls texture and depth—and eliminate the need for a lot of artwork—by covering them with Venetian plaster, a substance that is applied with a trowel and then burnished for a stucco-like effect.

70

One of the simplest ways to warm a modern interior (other than with a roaring fire) is with a soft, fluffy rug.

71

A few organic elements, such as the branch and plants used here, can also breathe life into a living room with a monochromatic palette—here, off-white.

72

Accents with reflective surfaces—a floor-to-ceiling mirror and crystal chandelier and table lamps—infuse a room with glamour. In this living area, serene, gray-blue furnishings ensure the look doesn't become too glitzy.

73

•

Here, limestone floors, white walls, and shaded floor-to-ceiling windows keep the atmosphere cool in the media room of a South Beach condominium.

74

Stock open shelves with clear glassware to keep a small pantry from feeling cluttered. Whitewashed cabinetry and a pale marble countertop contribute to the clean, airy vibe.

75

Imbue a mostly white kitchen with bright splashes of color—such as the green glass cabinet doors here. The geometric pattern of the Carrara marble–topped island is repeated on the slate floors and large window beyond.

76

Kitchen cupboards become like pieces of furniture when embellished with cornices and raised paneling. Here, the asymmetrical design of the panels—echoed in the stone floor tiles—lends a modern touch in keeping with the sleek stainless-steel appliances.

VIKING

77

Cool soapstone countertops and a honey-colored island help lighten a room dominated by rich, dark-wood cabinetry. Delicate hardware keeps the cupboards from feeling bulky. ◂

78

Small, pretty details—curved brackets, delicate muntins, gathered curtains—give kitchen cabinets feminine charm . . .

79

. . . that is kept in check by olive green paint and a glossy black soapstone backsplash and countertops.

80

Floating shelves, which take up less space than wall-mounted cabinets, are ideal in a narrow kitchen. Display only what you use regularly, along with a few decorative items, and relegate everything else to a cupboard or drawer.

81

Custom built-in millwork—here floor-to-ceiling shelves, sliding doors, lots of drawers, and a built-in desk with a walnut veneer—can transform a hallway into a sleek home office.

82

•

Cleaner than curtains and more decorative than shades, Shoji screens—here made of the same amber-colored wood as the door frames—soften the sunlight and set a zen tone.

83

•

Consider painting not just walls, but ceilings too, to magnify the color's impact. Here, the soothing qualities of lilac-gray make a room look more finished.

84

Nearly every surface in this dazzling, romantic bathroom shines: The walls are made of white milk glass, the cabinet doors feature mirrored panes, and the floor is lined with glass mosaic tiles. Even the woodwork gleams, thanks to high-gloss paint.

85

Cover not only a shower stall but also the wall beyond with aqua glass mosaic tiles to give a bathroom an ethereal, watery look. Here, the tiles also connect the transparent shower with the white soaking tub, making them feel less disjointed.

THE PHAIDON ATLAS
OF CONTEMPORARY WORLD ARCHITECTURE

86

You can enliven any room simply by arranging the furniture in unexpected ways. This asymmetrical walnut-aluminum-and-Plexiglas coffee table looks surprising in a space with rustic architecture; positioning the table so that it's perpendicular to the sofas and overhead beams gives it extra edge.

87

Make any living space—be it an entry, hallway, or family room—feel cozier by setting up a reading area. You don't need much: just a comfy chair, a warm throw, and a few books arranged on shelves or a table.

88

In a room with a stunning view, choose low, streamlined furnishings and let the view take center stage. Here, a glass cube coffee table—its shape echoed by boxy rope chairs—beautifully mirrors a sweeping window.

89

A graceful all-white entryway is an ideal canvas for a dark table with gorgeous lines, like this antique wood-topped metal piece. Its slanted legs and V-shaped support contrast nicely with the elegant turned balusters and vertical paneling.

90

•

If you really want to embrace simplicity, leave the white walls in a large room almost completely bare.

91

•

A collection of keenly edited furnishings can update a traditional room. Here, a refined settee is freshened with a subtle stripe and paired with armchairs covered in creamy solid fabrics. Set atop a sisal rug, they look elegant but not overly formal.

92

Create a light, airy scene with furnishings that seem to float: a coffee table with a clear base that disappears, a sofa with legs hidden behind a side table, a wall-mounted TV. Chairs with lots of space beneath them contribute to the breezy look.

93

Rustic teak benches are a great choice for a covered porch: They mix nicely with other wood finishes and upholstered pieces, and can be used for outdoor seating when needed.

94

•

Here's a fresh take on upholstery—covering not just seat cushions and backs, but legs (or arms) too. Whereas dark-wood chair legs would look chaotic beneath a table like this one, wrapping them in lime green fabric lets the elegant, five-prong stand shine.

95

•

A dining room need not be formal. Simple director's chairs—more commonly seen on patios or in game rooms—are an ideal match for a table with X-supports. The grid pattern on the canvas echoes the grilles on the windows, which are intentionally left bare to make the most of the view.

96

An armless sofa has the feeling of a banquette when pulled up to a breakfast room table. A trio of Lucite chairs is a pleasing counter point to the solid upholstery.

97

•

Design a dual-purpose space for dining and relaxing by pairing an unfussy, lightweight table (such as this bamboo one) and chairs with a long sofa. When it's not needed, the table can easily be moved aside.

98

Turn a beautiful table, like this antique one, into a charming bathroom countertop: have an opening cut for a drainpipe, purchase a vessel sink and faucets, and let a plumber do the rest.

99

•

Mix soft, richly tactile materials—a corrugated silk-wool rug, ultra-suede, and faille upholstery—to create a sumptuous, enticing effect.

100

•

The idea of crisp white upholstery is alluring, but in reality it's not always practical. Washable canvas slipcovers, used here on the sofa, chairs, and ottomans, are a low-maintenance solution.

101

•

Small details—such as the pretty, feminine pleats and gathered scalloped edges on this pair of Roman shades—become more important and noticeable in a spare space.

102

•

In a modern scheme, consider not only avant-garde styles but also innovative materials as well. This richly colored rug looks like shag, but it's actually made from felt.

103

•

By layering solid curtain panels over gauzy sheers, which tend to have a more delicate look than shades, you can give windows dimension and control the amount of light in a room.

Adventures With Old Houses

The SLOW MEDITERRANEAN KITCHEN
Recipes for the Passionate Cook
simply elegant napkin folding
HOTEL GEMS OF ITALY
Belvedere
HIDDEN GEMS OF TUSCANY
COASTAL LIVING COOKBOOK
the COASTAL LIVING COOKBOOK
Gourmet Shops of Paris
InStyle parties
PLAY
FOOD

104

A custom-made mantelpiece can add substance to the living room of a Mediterranean-style home. ◄

105

A buttery rug made of heavy wool sets a luxurious tone. Here, full, billowy curtains, ornate furnishings, and fringed pillows follow suit. ◄

106

In a room with dramatic architecture, curtains with a tasseled fringe provide a hint of embellishment without being over-the-top. Here, the rich hue of the fringe echoes the color of the arched beams above.

107

When designing a room, many interior decorators say they choose the carpet first because it makes subsequent decisions easier. Here, a colorful, graphic rug is the showpiece; the other furnishings are kept simple so as not to compete with it.

108

Subtle textures from sheer waffle-weave curtain panels, a linen-upholstered chair, and the brushstrokes on an abstract painting warm a creamy, minimalist space.

109

Infuse texture into an elegantly spare dining room with window treatments that feature subtle details. In this room, plain curtain panels are topped with pencil-pleats and their leading edges are trimmed with a long, luxurious trim.

110

Create a cohesive look by dressing all of the windows in a room—even French doors—with the same curtains. Mounting panels above the frame makes grandiose architecture, such as the doors shown here, appear even more magnificent.

Edward Weston

111

Unlike slipcovers or upholstery, curtains and throw pillows offer a relatively low-commitment way to incorporate pattern in a bedroom or any space. When you tire of them or the seasons change, simply trade them for something new.

112

Consider accenting a graceful four-poster with fabric-draped walls instead of a canopy. Generous pleats give the room texture without obscuring the bed's elegant shape.

113

•

Luxury doesn't have to be showy. A plush tufted bed frame and subtly patterned rug and chair, all in quiet shades of gray-blue and ivory, transform a bedroom into a dreamy, deluxe retreat.

114

•

Roman shades that can be drawn from the bottom up—permitting privacy without blocking light—are ideal in a ground-floor space. Narrow valances balance the look.

115

•

Pile birch logs vertically inside a fireplace (this one is constructed from smooth limestone) for a look that's both decorative and practical. Just rearrange the logs and remove any extras when you're ready to light a flame.

116

•

It's sometimes helpful to think of a room in terms of light and shadows. Here, bright white upholstery offsets a dark arrangement composed of primitive pottery, giant shells, and a heavy wooden table and carved mirror.

ROOMS

117

Some of the most intriguing displays don't cost a penny. Pinecones, birch logs, and twigs found in the yard and heaped into a wooden vessel soften a contemporary space.

118

Upholstered in Castel's Zoe, a lustrous fabric in a lively chartreuse hue, the sculptural lines of this beautiful nineteenth-century English settee stand out. Bolsters covered in the same fabric add another elegant touch.

119

Take care not to overdo a theme. In this living room, a pair of fanciful carved wooden seahorses and a bowlful of shells—set atop a pale cypress cabinet—are all that's needed to create a breezy, beachy vibe.

120

•

An ornate fireplace needs little adornment. In this room, a simple Art Deco mirror—whose protruding shape complements that of the mantel—unfussy sconces, and a smattering of accessories are just right.

121

•

An appealing vignette depends not just on the beautiful items you choose, but also on how you arrange them. In this scenario, a pair of square pillows echoes the shape of the gilded mirror, while the rectangular pillow mimics the lines of the antique striped bench.

122

Keep small vases on a mantel or table and continually rotate in blooms and branches—such as this trio of leaning orchid branches—from the garden or market.

123

Here's one way to chart a new decorating course. Divide an oversize map—here an antique map of Paris—into equal sections. Frame each piece and reassemble them on a wall for a stunning display.

PAUL HIMMEL

124

●

Architectural salvage companies are great places to look for interesting flourishes that can be used in lieu of artwork—such as this eighteenth-century Corinthian column.

125

●

Use bold shapes sparingly. In this kitchen, the carved wood posts, curved doorway, and range hood create a distinct and beautiful look.

WOLF

126

Just because a kitchen is a workspace doesn't mean it has to be void of artistic touches. These pendant lamps are a perfect blend of form and function, providing elegant modern shapes and focused light over a countertop. ◄◄

127

Narrow mirrors mounted over separate washbasins make a small bathroom ideal for two. The glass reflects light from the adjacent shaded sconces.

128

The glassy surface of an infinity pool set against a woodsy backdrop doubles the beauty of the surroundings.

129

Al fresco spaces, such as this rooftop terrace done up in bright pink hues, are good spots to experiment with daring colors. ▶

130

An all-weather carpet cuts down on glare from floor tiles and lays the foundation for a welcoming outdoor room. ▶

131

A streamlined pool house clad in cedar boards doesn't intrude on a leafy landscape. The structure's beauty—the varying colors of the wood, the way a louvered canopy casts slanted shadows on the facade—is natural and understated.

132

Convert a deck outside the master bedroom of a weekend house into an outdoor shower. Here, the deck is framed by a tall cast-concrete wall on one side and an unfinished cedar wall equipped with the showerhead on the other.

133

●

Weathered teak benches and dining chairs appear almost camouflaged when arranged on gray stone ledges, offering a natural backdrop for a pool. Here, the irregular stones complement the pool's amorphous shape.

134

●

Get creative in your garden. Flowers needn't be grown in a bed or planter—here, *Verbena bonariensis* spring through an opening in the center of a millstone. ►

135

●

In a sprawling yard, keep things simple by planting low-maintenance flowers that don't need much tending to. ►►

Chapter 3 Impact

• 142 • • 146 • • 149 • • 157 • • 164 •

• 167 • • 174 • • 179 • • 185 • • 190 •

• 196 • • 200 • • 206 • • 213 • • 217 •

YOU CAN HAVE a room filled with beautiful things, but if it doesn't have that unexpected touch, that wow factor, it might still fail to make an impression. Remember the old Duke Ellington song, "It Don't Mean a Thing (If It Ain't Got that Swing)"? You might think of your space that way and aim to infuse it with a bold, rhythmic pattern, on the walls, ceiling, or floor. Or go for a singular, more nuanced gesture: a vibrant, contemporary painting in a traditionally furnished room or a gorgeous, salvage door hung on the wall like art. Some dramatic ideas—such as painting the panels on a formal fireplace a bright or contrasting hue—cost next to nothing to create, and yet, as Ellington put it, they provide that "something else that makes the tune complete."

136

Create the feeling of two distinct spaces by painting the walls above and below a staircase in different colors.

137

In a traditional room with mahogany paneling, one expects a solid, creamy ceiling, perhaps dressed up with an elaborate fixture—which is exactly why the playfully patterned ceiling in this room is so striking.

138

A floor painted with concentric squares in sandy hues provides a neutral yet energetic canvas for colorful furnishings. The soft shapes of the splashy blooms and button-tufting are a nice counterpoint to the geometric design.

139

Make a bold statement by pitting two contrasting patterns against each other. One way to do it successfully is to assign a color palette to each print—here red and beige for the stripes and black and white for the checkerboard—then mix and match as you please.

140

From wooden ceiling coffers lined with woven cane to ribbed leather ottomans, nearly every surface in this Moroccan-inspired media room is infused with pattern and texture. It works because the motifs conform to a defined color palette and are all relatively small in scale.

141

Bet you never thought of burlap as elegant. But that's just the way it appears when hand-stenciled and applied to the walls of this living room. The cloth's rich texture and honey shade warm the lofty space.

142

Update a traditional fireplace with contrasting paint and tiles. Here, decorative panels have been painted in glossy black. The shape and shades of the tiles inspired the colors for the wall and ceiling.

143

Venetian plaster, popularly used in the palaces of fifteenth-century Venice, conveys a sense of majesty when combined with formal furnishings and gilt accessories. Here, the finish is paired with matching wainscoting for added interest.

144

An outdoor motif—such as the lattice-print on the sideboard and hand-painted walls of this cheerful dining room—looks fresh in a formal space. The plaid chair backs and subtle squares on the floor echo the geometric design.

145

Reinvigorate a classic wallpaper print, such as this toile, by installing it above wainscoting. Bright accents, like the lime green paint used on the back of a bookshelf, heighten the effect.

146

Coordinate patterns on walls and floors for a polished, multidimensional feel—here, the oversize circular print on the wallcovering complements the small hexagonal floor tiles in this Mediterranean-inspired space.

147

Bright paint on the floor can put an original twist on a traditional pattern—such as the folk art hex sign shown here—and keeps a country-style room from feeling quaint.

148

A striking collection deserves a proper perch. Here, colorful antique porcelain hens roost on a shelf rimming a breakfast nook, as well as in niches between windows. A wirework basket that was converted into a chandelier reinforces the country theme.

149

A tiled checkerboard backsplash brings retro punch to a kitchen. A recessed shelf treated with the same pattern is practically indiscernible and has the effect of an optical illusion.

150

With a little imagination, a piece designed for one purpose can be tasked with another. This gorgeous marble counter, found at a salvage shop, was once used for storing and serving ice cream at a diner.

151

A traditional print, such as this pineapple one, becomes modern when used in a large scale. Understated, organic colors and materials allow the motif to take center stage.

152

Give a den the feeling of a contemporary hunting lodge with faux-bois wallpaper and an artful display of antlers. (These were purchased at an online auction.) Dark wood and other natural materials enhance the look.

153

Create the dreamy look of an enchanted forest in a bedroom with a lush vine motif on the walls. This design is hand-painted, but wallpaper would work equally well. Slanted surfaces give the print a three-dimensional appearance.

154

Wallpaper with a bold, busy print, such as this toile, softens the edges of an irregularly shaped room. Papering a recessed nook offers a cozy spot for a desk.

155

Rich textures (such as this grasscloth ceiling) and patterns (leopard-print, plaids, stripes, florals) spice up a strict three-color palette.

156

Evoke the sense of having a canopy of blossoms overhead by papering the walls and sloped ceiling in a bedroom with a pretty floral print. Vases of fresh blooms and flowering branches enhance the effect.

157

Rows of mirrored panels make a sophisticated alternative to a headboard. These mirrors are silvered, which lends an aged, smoky patina.

158

Wallpaper rendered in soft shades and with lots of space between motifs—such as this hand-painted garden scene—has a relaxing effect that's ideal for a bedroom.

159

A swirling mosaic pattern on the floor makes a whitewashed bathroom come alive. The curved lines of the light fixture reiterate the motif, while the large photograph fleshes out the nature theme. ◄◄

160

Make the most of natural light in a bathroom by covering surfaces with a highly reflective material, such as the gleaming caramel-colored onyx seen here on the floors, tub deck, and walls of the double shower. ◄

161

When stripes are a dominant theme, as these contrasting limestone and marble ones are, opt for patterns that alternate narrow and wide bands. These tend to be more visually appealing than broad patterns of equal proportions.

162

Lessen the formality of a stately piece and the room it occupies with a casual display. On this antique secretary, old books, framed photos, and silver curios are arranged haphazardly on purpose.

163

A chaise longue is the ultimate comfy seat, but putting more than one in a room isn't always practical. Here, a quartet of more compact chairs with reclining backs and long seats lets several people relax at once.

PAUL HIMMEL
STUDIOS BY THE SEA
MICHAEL DWECK

164

The most intriguing furnishings often come from humble beginnings. This dramatically curved tufted settee was bought for a song at a thrift store and reupholstered in eye-catching floral ticking.

165

Be flexible when mounting pictures above a piece of furniture. Whereas a traditional row or square of frames would seem odd paired with this heart-shape settee, a grouping that echoes its form looks just right.

166

A leafy chintz, with all of its intricate details—shadows, subtle color variations, tiny veins and stems—lights up when set against dark walls.

167

Give a beautiful dining set the attention it deserves by contrasting it with its surroundings. This elegant whitewashed table and chairs shine in a room with scarlet walls and heavy, patterned curtains.

168

Transform a workaday picnic table into a chic indoor dining table. Here, one is painted a shiny lime green. Its benches are topped with chocolate brown cushions and pleated skirts trimmed with matching green braid.

169

Everyone gathers in the kitchen, so install a table that doubles as a work surface and a casual place to dine. This fourteen-foot-long marble-topped piece with stools arranged on two sides serves both purposes beautifully.

170

A patterned table made from a synthetic material, such as this pretty laminate one, is a smart touch in a kitchen. You'll never need a tablecloth, and the surface is a breeze to clean and care for.

WOLF
GOURMET

MUSIC

171

Red can energize just about any space. To keep it from feeling racy in a traditional room, combine it with classic patterns and materials like the plaids and crewel fabric in this library.

172

Cool blue unites a range of patterns—boldly striped armchairs, polka-dot curtains, delicately embellished tiles and china—in this seductive bedroom nook.

WORLD MYTHOLOGY
EN MARY JAMES STEELE
flowers exposed

173

●

This headboard scales new heights. Made of mahogany and embellished with a nickel grid that ties in with the metal on the spiky lamps, it stretches from floor to ceiling, bringing drama to a bedroom.

174

●

Here are two novel ideas: a wrap-around upholstered headboard that neatly embraces a bed as well as its side tables; and a footboard-cum-settee that masterfully blends form and function.

175

•

Curtains with linings have a dramatic, full look, provide insulation, and resist fading better than unlined styles. Viewed from the outside, a lining also tends to be more visually appealing than the reverse side of a pattern.

176

•

Consider this fresh way to play with pattern: Place a small, narrow-stripe rug, slightly askew, over a larger carpet with bigger stripes. Add colorful upholstery and throw pillows in a variety of motifs (plaid, leopard print) for a vibrant, eclectic look.

ORANGERIES

177

Instead of a coffee table, try using a pair of giant floor pillows (these feature an eye-catching embroidered design) to anchor a seating area. The cushions can hold board games or drinks on a tray and serve as extra seating when needed.

178

Make a small window feel larger by hanging curtains several inches away from the frame on either side, as seen on the right in this photo.

179

Showcase beautiful quilts—and bring extra layers of color and warmth to upholstered furnishings—by draping the coverlets over a sofa or large ottoman.

WAYNE THIEBAUD

180

Just because you've chosen an elaborately patterned rug doesn't mean the furnishings you pair with it have to be solid or neutral. Stripes and florals, drawn from the carpet's palette, can also work harmoniously.

181

Vibrant colors and patterns add drama to a double-height living room. Here, boldly patterned fabrics pep up a wing chair and a French neoclassical daybed. Velvet curtains and a red area rug add energy to the mix of antique furnishings.

182

Complement a lavishly intricate rug, such as this Persian one, with other opulent pieces: billowy curtains, tufted cushions, a crystal chandelier, an elaborately painted mirror.

183

Canvas trim gives these bright, richly textured chenille Roman shades a crisp, modern edge. The shape goes well with clean, utilitarian-style windows.

BAROQUE PAINTING

184

A band of cornflower-blue silk at the base of a luminous pale blue silk shade adds weight and keeps the light fabric from getting lost beneath abundant patterned curtains.

185

The most luxurious window treatments and bed canopies have hems that pool slightly on the floor. For an extravagant drape, choose curtains with a combined width of about three times that of the window.

186

Give bed canopies a charming, layered look with contrasting fabrics. A column of embroidered cloth lined with a cheerful check—which matches the headboard and footboard—crowns a twin bed in this cozy guest room.

187

Less expected than wallpaper or paint, fabric-covered walls lend texture and warmth to a room. Choose a pretty, printed design, like this Indian one, and you won't need many other decorations or artwork.

188

Here's an alternative to artwork in a frame: mounting a gorgeous fabric behind a canopy bed. Here, a shimmery, mirrored canopy and quilted silk coverlet provide dazzling counterpoints to the matte cloth.

189

A waterfall of box-pleated silk creates a glamorous backdrop for a bed. The one in this room is hung from a cornice cleverly aligned with the ceiling molding.

190

•

Sometimes a room designed around simple themes—primary colors, geometric shapes—has the greatest visual impact. Here, the angular lines of the bed and box-pleated valances stand in stark contrast to the rounded forms of the tables, as well as the lamps and circles on the rug.

191

•

Make store-bought items your own. In this young boy's room, a custom padded Ultrasuede headboard softens a streamlined steel bed.

192

Bring near-Eastern flair to a bedroom with a large-scale paisley pattern, a motif that originated in Persia. Delicate fringe adds softness to the curtains and canopy, which also features a fleecy chenille liner.

193

Give any bed the stature and softness of a canopied four-poster by installing gathered panels topped with a valance around the headboard. A luxurious velvet lining provides the curtains with weight and fullness.

JACKIE
OSCAR DE LA RENTA

194

Give a beautiful lamp greater presence with a well-placed mirror. The elegant mirror in this photo reflects a striking iron-and-glass chandelier from the nineteenth century. Truncated columns topped with hydrangea-filled tin urns contribute to the grand look.

195

A classically furnished room doesn't require a Wyeth or Renoir. Contemporary art, especially a colorful piece juxtaposed against neutral surroundings, also shines. ▶

196

Add a temporary new color—here green—to a room's palette by coordinating matching flowers and even fresh fruit. ▶

MANHATTAN

197

•

Never mind that your home didn't come with decorative molded panels and other distinctive details. Create your own grand architectural elements by hanging a beautiful salvage piece, like this eighteenth-century carved Italian door.

198

•

Distinguished architecture calls for accessories of the same caliber, such as a textural relief wall sculpture instead of framed pictures, or a folding screen covered in rich leather rather than more conventional fabric.

54

199

Draw attention to collectibles by displaying them in a glass case. This one, with a vibrant slatted-wood background, harmonizes with the vertical lines of the paneling on the walls, ceiling, and floor, and the striped rug.

200

Use accessories to dress up and define an unadorned fireplace. Here, an ornate antique carved-wood mirror is placed at about mantel-height, while a pair of floor lamps delineates a hearth.

201

A grouping of like artifacts from different cultures—here ornate Mexican crosses and a selection of Italian ex-votos—makes for a dynamic tabletop display.

202

Instead of covering all of the walls in a room with hand-painted wallpaper, which can be pricy, consider framing pieces from a single roll or remnant and using them as art. Gorgeous fabric panels also work well.

203

Handsome ceiling fixtures, which draw the eye up, can be used to highlight interesting architecture such as moldings, a pretty tin pattern, or in this case, a network of exposed beams.

204

A photograph makes a bold statement when enlarged to mural-size. This one was cut into pieces and reassembled, creating a grid with graphic, modern appeal.

205

Artwork with a soft, repeating motif (Cy Twombly's *Roman Notes,* shown here, resembles a handwritten missive) is a lovely foil for geometric-pattern upholstery.

206

A selection of whale vertebrae might be among the last things you'd expect to see arranged beneath an elegant glass chandelier, but the glamorous-meets-gritty look is surprisingly appealing.

207

Chinoiserie pieces have a sophistication that allows them to blend effortlessly with traditional decor. Here, an intricate copper lantern and a collection of ginger jars and other Asian-inspired objects infuse a dining room with romance.

208

A luminous clear-glass chandelier appears even more ethereal floating above a landscape of dark-wood furnishings. A pale oak table balances the look.

209

You can build a whole room around one gorgeous piece. A brilliant antique Guatemalan water container, used to hold blankets, influenced the color of the walls, duvet cover, and artwork in this blissful guest bedroom.

210

Need an easy, inexpensive way to display art en masse? Cut pictures, such as these illustrated nature studies, from a book and arrange them in frames. A black-and-white photo of leopard cubs harmonizes with the fanciful yet refined scheme in a young boy's room.

211

When it comes to sheer glamour, nothing beats Art Deco–style mirrored pieces. Match them with antiques, such as the bergère here, for a luxurious look in a bathroom or bedroom. ◄◄

212

Hang a large decorative mirror to brighten a dark bathroom. It will reflect natural light during the day and, in this room, the dazzling glow from a crystal chandelier at night. ◄

213

A giant, decorative mirror—of the sort more commonly seen in a living or dining area—looks fresh in a bathroom. Its reflective surface also helps expand the dimensions of a small space.

214

Your home is supposed to bring you joy, so go ahead and indulge your whims. In this pool house, a quirky "Funny Boy" sign and pen-and-ink drawing of the actor Nathan Lane pay homage to *The Producers.*

215

An old barn can be transformed into a stunning space for an indoor pool. This structure, which boasts its original Pennsylvania bluestone walls, is furnished with comfy wicker pieces.

216

•

You can make a big splash in a small backyard: consider this modern checkerboard patio framed by a rose-edged lily pond.

217

For an exalted look, try installing an arcade, like this teak one, and covering it with a variety of light-filtering, climbing blooms such as wisteria, clematis, and roses.

218

Like rooms, gardens don't have to conform to one style. A mix of shrubs, ferns, grasses, water-loving fronds, even a tall 'Green Arrow' Weeping Alaskan cedar, infuse this scene with personality.

Chapter 4 Function

• 223 • • 227 • • 231 • • 232 • • 238 •
• 245 • • 257 • • 260 • • 269 • • 272 •
• 275 • • 280 • • 284 • • 291 • • 297 •

IF YOU'VE EVER LOOKED at the expertly designed rooms in a decorating book or magazine and thought "yeah right, that would never work in *my* home," this chapter is for you. While it's wonderful to have a gorgeous space with dramatic flair, you still have to live there. Luckily, there are plenty of tricks you can employ to make a room both beautiful and practical. Have a busy (or boisterous) family? Learn about scratch-resistant stone, durable upholstery fabric, and smart storage solutions. Short on space? Set up a home office or library in an existing room or underutilized nook. Need a place to zone out at the end of the day? Create the serene, sumptuous bedroom you've always dreamed of. Now *that's* what life is all about.

219

•

Cover a playroom wall with chalkboard paint to ensure the surface is ready whenever inspiration strikes young artists. Other smart touches include pint-size furniture and a beige cotton carpet that camouflages minor stains.

220

•

Wall paneling, which is readily available at home supply stores, is an easy way to bring character to a room lacking architectural details.

221

Rich, espresso-brown walls, set off by bright white doors and trim, envelop a casual dining area in warmth. In this room, textured bamboo shades and a sisal rug bridge the contrasting hues.

222

When it comes to creating an elegant look, less is often more. Graceful, dark-wood furnishings, simple striped seats, and a coat of khaki-colored paint on the walls make this room beautiful and livable.

223

Keep wood floors gleaming with occasional damp mopping. (Never saturate the surface with water.) Most wood floors are finished with polyurethane, a protective coating, and don't need to be waxed. Unfinished floors, or those treated with varnish or shellac, should be waxed once or twice a year.

Wine
WINE

224

Think of solid surfacing materials, such as the pale green Corian on this island, as the ultimate in luxurious yet low-maintenance countertop options. These man-made surfaces look like stone but require no polishing, sealing, or special cleaners. They come in a wide range of colors.

225

No room for a home office? Create one in the kitchen or any area with a wall available for installing a desk, shelves, and a few cabinets. Choose colors and materials that coordinate with the rest of the room.

226

Maximize kitchen storage with cabinets that stretch to the ceiling. Incorporating both solid and window cupboards enables you to display beautiful items and hide utilitarian ones.

227

A red checkerboard floor and cabinets finished with crimson glaze bring vibrance and personality to this kitchen.

228

Built-in appliances—including a refrigerator and freezer covered with the same wood paneling as the cabinets—keep a kitchen looking clean and orderly. ▶

229

Simplicity is crucial in a tight space. Here, bead-board on the walls and ceiling provide a clean backdrop for white cabinets—designed to mimic the window—and drawers. Even the dishes are white, adding to the light, airy look.

230

•

Enclosing a small kitchen with an open shelving system makes everything easily accessible. Here, covered niches below eye level provide space for odds and ends such as timers, spoon rests, and salt and pepper mills.

231

Pietra Cardosa, a type of schist used here on the countertops and backsplash, offers the beauty of soapstone but is harder and more resistant to scratches. Somewhat porous, this stone should be sealed a few times a year.

232

Wouldn't it be nice if you didn't have to display the mixer, toaster, or knife block, let alone take up precious counter space with them? A kitchen catchall and workspace like the one here lets you conceal those items—and myriad others—but still keep them at your fingertips.

233

•

You don't need a whole room to devote to a library. Floor-to-ceiling shelving can transform even a small space, such as this alcove, into a cozy spot for books. Adjustable shelves are convenient for stowing volumes of different sizes, and good lighting is key.

234

•

A built-in bead-board bench topped with a cushion provides a great perch for removing shoes in a mudroom. Add hooks for bags and umbrellas and open shelves with baskets for smaller items.

▶

235

Metal lockers and plenty of hooks help organize miscellaneous items in a garage so that you can easily find what you're looking for.

236

Consider applying an epoxy floor coating over concrete in a garage. This creates a shiny surface that is stronger—and more attractive—than concrete alone and is easier to clean.

237

You might not think to put a loveseat in a hallway unless you knew how invigorating a pop of bright upholstery could be there. This antique piece is newly covered in a vibrant stripe.

238

•

Here's a clever idea: convert a beautiful salvage window into a coffee tabletop, as was done in this room with a nineteenth-century Indian wood-and-glass piece.

239

•

The main ingredient for a comfy living room? A sofa—or two—you can sink into. These overstuffed, pillow-laden ones fill the bill. Fuzzy tables (that almost resemble lapdogs!) enhance the luxurious, welcoming vibe.

240

Create a cohesive yet eclectic look by upholstering furnishings in variations on the same hue. The palette in a collection of pear prints inspired the green and brown pieces, including a two-tone sofa, in this room. Notice how different the two armchairs appear—one in lime, the other in forest green.

241

With a throw casually draped over the top, this upholstered coffee table is treated like a sofa or chair, giving the room a warm, easeful quality.

242

Small, easy-to-move rattan pieces make it easy to rearrange a living room for work or socializing.

243

A pair of vintage leather wing chairs, each with its own reading lamp, brings the cozy feeling of a den to a crisp white parlor.

244

Instead of the traditional sofa-armchair-coffee table scenario, consider pulling a dining table up to a banquette in a living room. This offers a more functional space for conversing, working, or casual dining.

245

A dual-purpose room, such as this living and dining space, calls for dual-purpose pieces. These patterned furnishings are pretty enough to display in an elegant setting, and the chairs comfortable enough to pull out for extra seating in the living area.

246

To encourage conversation in a dining space, opt for a round table and sumptuous chairs like these upholstered in a mohair-velvet fabric. A low table arrangement ensures everyone can make eye contact.

247

A dining room doesn't have to house a dining set. Mixing stained and painted pieces, such as this nineteenth-century walnut table and whitewashed chairs from the same period, looks chic.

248

Garden furniture looks beautiful in almost any sunny, casual spot, whether indoors or out. In this breakfast nook, scrolled French benches flank an antique farm trestle table.

249

•

If you have small children or otherwise expect furnishings to endure a lot of wear and tear, durable, easy-to-clean cotton or synthetic upholstery is your best bet. Patterned fabrics, such as this plaid, tend to hide stains better than solid cloths.

250

•

Consider having a new piece professionally aged to match older furnishings. This reproduction dining table was treated so that it would have the same worn, mellow sensibility as the 1920s lyre-back chairs that surround it.

POIS
TO MOM
YOU'RE THE BEST
I LOVE YOU
A LOT

251

•

If you have a large family to entertain, consider setting up a seating area at one end of an open kitchen. This gives people a place to gather apart from the workspace, while allowing the cook to socialize.

252

•

In a small apartment kitchen, a round table on wheels can be pulled up to a built-in bench for dining or pulled over to the counter for extra prep space.

253

Rattan furniture—here paired with splashy floral prints—lends a warm, tropical vibe to any kind of room. To keep the pieces looking great, vacuum regularly, as dust accumulates in the textured surfaces.

254

Let the style of a room spill out into a hallway. Here, soft green upholstery and a playfully patterned pillow connect a sophisticated settee, flanked by a Victorian marble-topped table, to the child's room next door.

255

Sometimes a couple of gorgeous pieces in a captivating color are all a room requires. Such is the case in this guest bedroom, where vintage carved wooden beds painted an electrifying blue take center stage.

256

Instead of a chest or bench, consider installing a comfortable sofa at the foot of a bed. Placing small bureaus as bedside tables is another unexpected touch—think of all the storage you'll gain.

257

For an attractive yet functional display on open shelves, store odds and ends in handsome boxes, such as these rattan ones, and keep magazines in vertical files. Scatter a few decorative items throughout and—voilà!

258

Design a bedroom that strikes a pleasing balance between plush and rustic with dramatic, floor-grazing fabrics in homey prints, such as plaids and florals.

259

A canopy bed can be just as beautiful without a canopy. This bed's slender skeleton harmonizes wonderfully with the lines on an antique bamboo desk chair and armoire.

260

•

Constructed around a window, built-in closets, drawers, and open shelves along one wall of a bedroom create generous storage, improve the proportions of the long, narrow room, and form the foundation of a small window seat.

261

•

Plentiful furnishings in dark and medium hues (navy blue, honey brown) help ground a room with a pale, sweeping ceiling, as illustrated in this photo of a pool house's vaulted, post-and-beam ceiling.

262

A crisp paneled tablecloth, in keeping with the formality of an entrance hall, offers a shot of color—and, beneath its skirt, a spot to stow shoes.

263

Instead of fulfilling a practical purpose, curtains can sometimes be used simply to frame a spectacular view.

264

You might not think to pair an Oriental rug with sunny, plaid curtains or a warm red, tan, and gold palette with a watery landscape, but the contrast works beautifully in this room.

265

A couple of alpaca throws warms a bleached palette that includes a sofa and chairs covered in easy-to-care-for muslin slipcovers and pale linen pillows.

266

•

One way to create an inviting, indulgent space: soften the edges. Here, gracefully gathered shades, a fabric-draped ottoman, skirted upholstery, and a dimpled banquette topped with a multitude of pillows all work to that effect.

267

•

Linen slipcovers are a smart choice for dining chairs since, unlike upholstery, they can be removed and washed after a spill. It's worth investing in custom covers, as ready-made ones tend to be ill fitting, especially on unusually shaped furniture.

268

For a laid-back look, choose billowy, unlined curtains—which tend to filter light rather than block it—in a cheerful print like this sunny stripe. Go for sleek hardware and avoid fussy valances and swags.

269

•

Give classic, ladder-back chairs feminine flair with pretty skirted covers. A printed-fabric valance and lampshades provide contrast while continuing the ladylike theme.

270

Here are two things you don't see very often in a kitchen: throw pillows and an elegantly draped patterned valance. But in this refined space, with its window seat and shiny marble countertops, they are perfectly appropriate.

271

Gathered check curtains, which offer a subtle counter-point to ornately patterned backsplash tiles, soften glass-front kitchen cabinets and tie them into the color scheme.

272

A window seat with an extra-thick cushion makes a cozy spot for napping in a study. If your space doesn't have or permit a seat like this, consider a daybed.

273

The remnants pile at the fabric store is a great place to look for beautiful, inexpensive cloths that are often just the right size for pillows. The ones shown here were all made with fabric scraps.

274

A scenic print, such as a toile, can work wonderfully with a geometric motif like a plaid or stripe. Try letting one pattern dominate, as the toile does here, and allow the other to serve as an accent.

275

When drawn closed, bed curtains block early morning light filtering through the window shutters. In this master bedroom, curtains made of warm wool plaid lined with a luxurious silk taffeta check, both from Christopher Hyland, are as functional as they are beautiful.

276

Vary a motif by using one fabric in different ways. On this porch, the same striped cloth that appears on the shades was cut and pieced back together to form another pattern on the throw pillows.

277

●

A series of framed black-and-white photographs has a contemporary, art gallery edge that contrasts beautifully with warm, weathered wood furniture.

278

For an intriguing tabletop display, compile different items of various sizes that you love. Here, a 1940s mercury glass lamp, vintage vases, and garden urns mingle effortlessly. The goose soaring overhead is a whimsical touch.

279

A mirror (or painting) and a smattering of vases from different eras, such as this creamy art glass one and a pair of colorful nineteenth-century papier-mâché pieces, dress up a simple mantel. Add flowers when you have them, but the vases also look stunning on their own.

280

•

One stellar object can inspire a whole palette: Here, the blue, gold, and pink in a lusterware pitcher influenced the room's upholstery.

281

Antique stores and flea markets offer myriad exquisitely crafted, formerly utilitarian pieces—painted sleds, textured washboards, metal watering cans—that can be displayed as art.

282

●

For maximum intimacy, hang a light fixture about three feet above a dining table. This guideline applies even in a soaring space like this breakfast nook.

283

Large antique Chinese pendant lanterns, of the sort more commonly seen in a living or dining area, bring sophistication to a kitchen. In this room, an ebonized table with Chinoiserie details reiterates the motif.

284

Beautiful china doesn't have to be kept behind glass, only to be brought out on special occasions. Arrange pieces—such as this dazzling French Quimper collection—on open shelving so they brighten every meal.

285

Collectibles, such as delicately painted teapots, become even more compelling when displayed together. Turned to the side, the rows of spouts form pleasing silhouettes.

286

When it comes to collecting, there are a few schools of thought. You can go after a certain style, such as the vibrant majolica displayed on an antique étagère in this kitchen . . .

287

. . . or you might amass miscellaneous pieces in a favorite hue, like the cherry-red seen here. To emphasize the theme, these shelves are painted a glossy scarlet.

288

Displayed out of context, in a bedroom or living area, a china collection takes on a grand, artistic sensibility. Here, blue-and-white dishes dotting plate rails in a garret are wonderfully unexpected.

289

Night tables needn't be identical. Here, different tables make the room less formal, while matching lamps establish a sense of balance.

290

A series of miniature compositions can sometimes be as appealing as a single large one. In this bedroom, arrangements of botanical prints and starburst mirrors are hung over the bed and night tables.

291

Ceramic garden stools, like these Chinese antiques, are wonderfully versatile in a sunroom or other living area. Use them as footstools, tables, waterproof plant stands, or extra seating at a party (keep some cushions handy).

292

If you collect items in a favorite color, you will always be able to put together a coordinated, striking display.

293

The most important ingredient needed to create a relaxing ambiance? Good lighting. Experiment with a mix of electric lighting and candlelight, such as the sconces (which don't need to match) and hurricane lamps seen here—until you find the right mood.

294

Make a long, narrow terrace feel cozy by setting up several different seating areas—here one for dining and another for relaxing.

295

A pergola furnished with a built-in grill, countertops, and cabinets (these are covered with gorgeous old cypress shutters) becomes a practical—and magical—outdoor kitchen.

296

An open-air pool house has the feeling of a cozy living room when appointed with indoor-style furnishings, including oversize floral pillows that were inspired by hydrangeas in the garden (now on the table).

297

Teak furniture and weather-proof acrylic upholstery—almost indistinguishable from cotton canvas—will weather nicely in the elements.

298

Define an outdoor seating area, and protect it from the elements, with curtains made of a heavy, durable material such as cotton duck (shown) or canvas. Contrasting trim makes the utilitarian fabric look decorative.

299

Giant terra-cotta pots filled with fruiting trees, herbs, and flowering plants in staggered sizes infuse a patio or courtyard with color and texture.

300

Bring beautiful patterns and a lovely aroma to a patio by planting greens such as sweet alyssum and creeping thyme between stones. This also contributes to a more natural look, since plants tend to sprout in these spots anyway.

301

An elegant gated arbor—here punctuating a fence draped with pink 'Sally Holmes' roses and bordered with purple larkspur—provides a focal point at the end of a garden path and a frame for a stunning view.

302

•

Design a garden with the sensibility of an Impressionist painting by planting blooms such as irises en masse and letting wildflowers (butter-cups, daisies) grow as they please. Viewed from a distance, the colors blend into magnificent pastel swaths.

303

•

On a large property, create a glorious patchwork by planting swaths of tall, unfussy grasses and flowers, such as purple asters and feathery, silvery pink *Miscanthus* 'Flamingo.'

Chapter 5 Details

• 302 •
• 309 •
• 317 •
• 320 •
• 325 •
• 326 •
• 331 •
• 332 •
• 334 •
• 337 •
• 339 •
• 342 •
• 347 •
• 350 •
• 354 •

THE PHRASE "God is in the details" is frequently attributed to Le Corbusier, one of the most influential architects in modern history. Consider a shiny row of decorative nail heads marching along the top of a camelback sofa, or the delicate tassels dangling from a curtain panel to understand immediately the big impact small touches can have. As you'll discover in this section, attention to particulars involves more than just choosing beautiful items. It's also about layering patterns and textures, and taking the time to upgrade those less-than-perfect pieces—whether re-covering pillows in gorgeous antique fabric or defining the edge of a cushion with silky fringe. You'll find some grand, yet still exquisitely refined, gestures here, too, such as the handpainted mural on page 305 and the embossed leather wall panels on page 312.

304

Who says doors can't be both utilitarian and decorative? A beautifully carved and stained set—Asian-inspired here—is practically a work of art.

305

•

Anchor a vignette of dishes, such as these bone china pieces, by setting one in a plate stand atop a gilded bracket. Mount the others with plate hangers so that they appear to float around it.

306

Create a sense of light and shadows on a wall by layering yellow-ochre paint over a browner hue. The glow from a candle bulb sconce, like the one made of forged iron here, heightens the blended effect.

A GOD WITHIN
CERVANTES
NABOKOV
NABOKOV
IN RUSSIA
THE STORY OF A LIFE
TOLSTOY

307

Distressed paint and beams made from salvaged timber infuse a living room with old-world appeal.

308

Instead of hanging a painting on the wall, consider painting the wall itself with a beautiful mural. Look for a local artist whose work you admire and ask if he or she will work on commission.

309

Borrow a trick from the upholstery world and tack the edges of a piece of fabric to a wall using close-set decorative nails. Enhance the elegant, custom look with curtains, seat covers, or a tablecloth in a matching print.

310

With their minute imperfections, hand-painted walls like these striped ones tend to have a friendlier feel than those dressed with wallpaper. Even stenciled designs can have a similar effect.

311

•

Intricately carved legs that mimic those on a nearby island lend an exquisite, furniture-like quality to a kitchen sink. Elegant hardware and a slim marble backsplash augment the refined feeling.

312

•

A marble checkerboard on a backsplash provides a graphic canvas for displaying shiny pots and pans, dishes, and utensils. ▶

313

•

A marble-topped table that extends from a kitchen island offers informal dining space and extra prep area when needed. ▶

314

A backsplash consisting of mosaic tiles arranged not randomly but in sleek stripes brings a tailored touch to a kitchen. A decorative arch over the range hood frames the motif.

315

Design a dynamic home office using a palette of brown. The key is to contrast textures—the grasscloth walls behind Shoji screens in this scenario—as well as colors. Note the lively combination of dark walnut and pale pine on the desk.

316

The ultimate luxurious wall covering? Warm, leather panels, like those in this library. The embossed damask pattern, which echoes that on an armchair, along with other fine details in the room—silky tassels, decorative nails—add to the feeling of indulgence.

317

Envelop a den, or other cozy space, with softness by covering the walls with rich, velvet fabric. For extra polish, this vibrant cloth is finished with grosgrain ribbon trimmed with decorative nails.

318

•

Sometimes one wall treatment just won't do—you need three. In this bedroom, molding, hand-stenciled wallpaper, and a swath of bright pink linen are a charming combination.

319

•

Many retailers reproduce antique wallpaper—such as this chrysanthemum pattern—making it easy and affordable to give a room a pedigreed look. A pair of bright, modern pillows provides contrast.

320

Give a room gorgeous architectural detail by layering latticework panels over walls painted a soft, pastel shade. This is perfect for a sunroom, where the lattice can add to a larger garden theme.

321

For a light, airy look, choose sofas and chairs with exposed legs, as opposed to skirted styles. Be sure to consider how the supports will work together with other pieces in the room. Here, claw feet contrast nicely with the angular lines of the coffee tables.

322

Think of upholstery trimmings as the jewelry that completes a beautiful outfit. Notice, for example, how decorative nails highlight the graceful curves of a Louis XV settee and how the thick, textured cord defines the cushion.

323

A muted color scheme and a discreet use of pattern keep the focus on the details, such as the lavender French stitching of these linen-slipcovered Dessin Fournir sofas.

HAMPTONS
ROYAL HOLIDAYS
LUCIEN HERVE
A HOUSE IS NOT A HOME Bruce Weber

324

Update a pair of armchairs by upholstering the frames in beige raffia and covering the seat cushions with pale blue mohair. As a finishing touch, trim the backs and arms with double rows of nailheads.

325

Mix warm and cool tones in unexpected ways: here, the walls are painted a soft cocoa brown, while the ceiling and the backs of the built-in bookshelves are a pale robin's egg blue.

326

•

Upholstery nails can be used in a variety of ways—positioned with no gaps between them, known as "close-nailing"; spaced slightly apart; or arranged in parallel rows, referred to as "double-" or "triple-nailing." For a lavishly embellished look, choose pieces, such as this sofa, that combine several techniques.

327

•

Neutral hues enable solid-, striped-, and floral-upholstered furnishings to mingle effortlessly. Pencil-thin piping on each piece also helps unite them.

328

Trimmings can be used for more than defining edges. This silk braid was sewn onto the face of a slipper chair, creating a delicate patterned border. Solid-hued piping provides the chair a crisp outline.

329

Paintings don't have to reside on walls: This hand-painted lattice-arabesque motif turns a television cabinet into an elaborate showpiece.

330

Silk balloon shades edged with a thick band of braid have the look of an elegant ball gown. In fact, in seventeenth-century Europe, when such trimmings were first used, the same kinds of ornaments that adorned upholstery also graced women's dresses.

331

An elegant space often calls for curtains, but when they are not feasible, as with a very narrow window, a structured fabric pelmet—this one is finished with contrasting braid—strikes just the right note.

332

Who knew felt could be so glamorous? Used to make the bands, loops, and fleur-de-lis that trim these lofty curtains, the fuzzy fabric complements the weight of the wool-silk panels and proves to be an elegant ornament indeed.

333

A boldly patterned rug that stretches almost the length of a room helps to define the color palette and unite different seating groups in a sweeping space.

334

•

Bands of checked fabric temper the formality of ivory pleated curtains. The country-style chandelier hung over the graceful table surrounded with Louis XIV–inspired chairs has a similar effect.

335

Encourage lingering over a meal by treating a breakfast nook banquette as if it were a sofa and piling on the pillows. A lazy Susan placed in the center of the table makes serving a breeze.

336

Give vertically striped curtains extra edge by finishing the leading sides with folded bands of the same fabric, turned horizontally.

337

The pattern play continues at the dining table in this room: note how unexpected a pair of living room–style wing chairs accented with striped pillows looks mixed with wooden chairs with floral crewelwork seats.

338

●

A tapestry—such as this English antique—has a neater, more polished look when stretched across panels, and mounted edge-to-edge. Achieve a similar effect with any beautifully patterned fabric. Here, a coverlet made from pieced-together vintage cloths complements the wall hanging.

339

●

Linen wall fabrics add an extra touch of comfort, coziness, and quiet to a guest bedroom.

AB

340

Sumptuous fabrics can bring texture to a monochromatic room. Here, a sofa, chair, and ottoman are upholstered in distressed palomino leather, promising instant relaxation to anyone who pauses for a rest.

341

Create an alluring nook for a bed by overlapping different fabrics. In this space, a toile panel and overhanging valance frame shiny satin pillows and a plush silk-velvet headboard. Artwork is hung on top of the curtain, contributing to the layered look.

342

Checked fabric has a tendency to look homespun—but not when it's gathered into an elaborate sunburst canopy finished with pencil-pleat panels. Matching lampshades and monogrammed linens heighten the sophistication.

343

Create balance in a room with lots of pattern by choosing one of the prints' non-dominant colors—in this case soft lavender—for the walls.

344

A custom duvet cover with a ruffled edge made from the same fabric adds luster to a master bedroom. Window treatments and a decorative pillow cover, also made from the same fabric, keep the look cohesive.

345

Familiar plaids and stripes are among the most comforting patterns. Keep them looking fresh by layering different styles of the same motif, as with the armchair, throw, and window shades in this bedroom.

346

Thick moss fringe, named for the velvety forest covering it resembles, lends a luxurious touch to pillows and cushions. This trimming looks especially appropriate in a nature-themed setting, like this sunroom.

347

Make a grand entrance by outfitting a front door with glamorous accents, such as beveled glass windows, and gracious architectural details, like columns and cornices.

348

For a brilliant display, try arranging colorful glass vases, such as these mid-century ones, so that they overlap on a windowsill. The pieces will look different depending on the direction of the sun, creating a kaleidoscopic effect.

349

Sometimes even clothing can be presented as art. Take this gauzy circa-1800 Chinese undergarment, which is mounted on a pole above a nineteenth-century elm grain chest, also from China.

350

Scour Web sites and online auctions for beautiful antique fabrics you can use for pillows. (The golden ones here were made with luxurious eighteenth-century cloth.) Old pieces have a warmth and personality that new fabric can't match. Just be sure to ask the seller about any holes or stains before making a purchase.

351

Hand-painted tiles turn an unremarkable fireplace into a work of art. These, which feature figurines in various action poses, lend a sense of playfulness and tie into a broader Chinoiserie theme.

352

A grouping of artwork need not be arranged symmetrically. These engravings, which complement the paneled architecture, show how refreshing an unbalanced display can be.

353

•

Take a traditional item, such as a chandelier, combine it with an unexpected material, like wooden beads (did you ever imagine they could look so elegant?), and you've got a spectacular showpiece.

354

•

Create a festive spirit at a dinner party by designing a table around a theme. Here, shell- and coral-adorned pieces lend a soft, beachy vibe.

355

•

The smallest details—a silk tassel dangling from a china cabinet key, openwork embellishment on a tablecloth, a bright ribbon cinching a napkin at a place setting—can make an elegant space feel even more gracious.

356

An old-fashioned look doesn't have to be rough-hewn. Pretty Delft tiles (which originated in The Netherlands in the sixteenth century), elaborately carved woodwork, and delicate hardware give a kitchen a classic, sophisticated air.

357

•

When designing centerpieces, think outside the flower garden (or market). Found items such as berries, branches, leaves, and seed-pods can all lend themselves to an intriguing, and unexpected, seasonal display.

358

A playful font and modern plaid fabric offer a welcoming message on a guest bedroom pillow.

359

Update traditional architecture in a bathroom with ultra-modern fixtures—such as this sleek, freestanding faucet—and sophisticated touches like museum-style lighting over a pair of peaceful landscape paintings.

360

Brighten a gazebo or covered porch with a frieze. In this photo, a Matisse-inspired motif of frolicking swimmers is painted on interior beams. A graphic wallpaper border would also give the same effect.

361

You can treat outdoor teak furnishings, like this bench and pair of chairs, with a sealer or oil to maintain their original amber color, but why bother? The pieces naturally fade to a silver-gray that is just as beautiful.

362

●

Add a splash of color to a garden or yard with low-maintenance blooming perennials—such as the *Persicaria* 'Firetail' here.

Chapter 6 Color

• 360 • • 364 • • 368 • • 372 • • 385 •

• 389 • • 390 • • 396 • • 401 • • 406 •

• 410 • • 414 • • 418 • • 420 • • 431 •

IT'S NOT SURPRISING that many people are intimidated when choosing colors. With all the subtle shades and potentially endless combinations available, it may seem hard to know where to start. But nothing sets the tone of a room like color. Red, for example, is so powerful that studies have shown that the mere sight of it can cause one's heart to beat faster, while pink has proven to have a sedative effect. Cool blues tend to create a soothing, calm, and relaxed atmosphere, while neutral colors simply allow the other colors in a room to take center stage. When coming up with a palette, consider not only what mood you want to create, but also the shades that please you. Think about the clothes you like to wear, the artwork you favor, and the places you love to visit. The rich scarlets, oranges, and golds in a favorite painting or the neutral sand and sea shades of the beach can be a launching point for an entire scheme.

363

Rich, velvety-red walls make a small formal room feel positively regal (and a china collection pop). Choose a flat paint finish, rather than glossy, which tends to look more racy.

364

When you have a room painted a bold color, keep the palette of adjoining spaces relatively neutral.

365

Another unexpected way to inject color is to paint the steps of a staircase. A runner, here with vibrant stripes, protects the paint from wear.

366

Paint a room an eye-popping shade and you've actually made choosing furnishings easier, since neutrals are often the best bet in this scenario. Tie the look together with a few accents that match the walls, such as the pillow and desk accessories seen here.

367

Rooms in an open floor plan don't have to be decorated the same way, but they should coordinate. Here, the bright orange in pairs of striped curtains is just enough to connect the space to the adjoining color-drenched living area.

368

For a warm, mottled glow—rather than a shock of saturated color—apply golden paint over walls finished with rough plaster.

369

Are you attracted to vivacious hues but wary of using them in an entire room? Consider painting just the ceiling—in this room, a lime green—and balancing it with a sprinkling of bright furnishings and accessories.

370

Life imitating—or mingling with—art can produce a sensational effect. In this dining room, a Chinese ginger jar echoes one in the hand-painted wallpaper, while a delicate sconce looks as though it were part of an illustrated chandelier.

371

Elaborately patterned wallpaper, like this floral print, offers a wealth of shades to choose from when selecting furnishings. In this hallway, pink, green, blue, and gold pieces work beautifully together.

372

Muted metallic wallpaper is a brilliant choice for any light-filled space—even a study. To keep it from feeling showy, choose neutral-hued furniture and rustic accents, such as the barn star and chandelier seen here.

373

●

If you have different types of walls in the same room, consider painting just one kind of surface, as was done with the board-and-batten here. This provides a glorious shot of color (without painting the whole room) and makes the varying architecture seem more deliberate.

374

Give a new living space the homey feeling of a generations-old barn by installing rusticated wood beams and a pair of sliding doors painted a vibrant shade.

375

Think red for a dining room. Here, a wall of bookshelves—painted with high-gloss Chinese red and decorated with eighteenth-century Italian engravings—sets off eighteenth-century silver-gilt armchairs and a round mahogany table.

THE ART OF GREECE
PONTORMO
ROME
Anthony van Dyck Drawings
THE SISTINE CHAPEL
THE LAUNDRYMEN
HITLER
CENTURY

376

Silvery and white touches—such as pewter chandeliers, a large contemporary mirror with a silver-gilt frame, and white-painted shutters—set off the rich blue walls and secure a fresh mood in this traditional dining room.

377

For a gorgeous, two-tone look, install wainscoting around the perimeter of a room, and then paint the rest of the walls and the ceiling a bright hue. The narrow band of color provides a great place to showcase artwork, as in this room.

378

When your color scheme says one thing—here, cheerful blue-and-white has a French provincial flavor—and your furnishings another—the new dark-wood furnishings look contemporary—you've got an exciting mix.

379

Create a refreshingly bold look in a kitchen by painting not just cabinets, but also their interiors and moldings, with a dazzling shade. Uninterrupted by white space, the color packs a serious punch.

380

●

Increase the vivaciousness in a kitchen with a mosaic tile backsplash made up of bright yellow, red, and orange tiles mixed with a sprinkling of more calming colors, such as lavender and olive green.

381

Have you ever dreamed of using three or more colors of paint in one room? You might get tired of these schemes in a living area, but an out of the way spot, such as a laundry room, is a great place to live out a color fantasy.

382

•

Strié is a streaked design created by dragging a brush through glaze applied over a base color. Thanks to its subtlety, this treatment—here rendered in luminous pale peach—is easy to match with other patterns.

383

•

Keep cheerful, country-style motifs (checks, quilt patterns) from feeling chintzy by choosing prints in a single fresh shade, such as the spring green seen here.

384

White comes in hundreds of shades—some slightly blue, others more gray, pink, or gold. To find the right one, compare paint chips with the other colors in the room. Here, furnishings painted a warm, apricot-tinged white are a perfect match for tawny walls.

385

Fabrics and wallpaper printed with a classic American buffalo check create a sense of welcome in a guest bedroom. A pale sophisticated color, such as beige, prevents the homespun pattern from appearing kitschy.

386

Colors don't have to be bright to be effective. Textured, gray-blue wallpaper and matching toile linens turn this bedroom into a sumptuous escape.

387

A blue shade, such as that in this mosaic tile, is a wonderfully soothing choice for a bathroom. Given the color of the grout, white is a natural accent. Play up the scheme with snowy marble surfaces and a speckled floor that incorporates both hues.

388

White walls and bare windows are anything but dull when juxtaposed with furnishings in rich, saturated colors and varying materials, such as the mohair-velvet sofa and leather-and-wrought iron chairs in this living area.

389

An array of differently upholstered seating can lend an air of sophistication to a living room—if the color palette is limited to few colors, here blue, pink, and green.

390

Color helps make formal furnishings feel more inviting, an effect that is even more pronounced when the pieces are upholstered in soft, tactile materials, such as the blue suede, brown cotton-velvet, and pink velveteen seen here.

391

•

Enliven a sedate, two-tone palette with a variety of patterns (florals, checks, dots), contrasting trimmings, and other pretty details such as button-tufting or decorative nail heads.

392

•

Infuse soft hues, such as aqua and pink, with energy by combining them with an arresting pattern. To keep the look consistent, not busy, repeat one motif throughout the room. Here, the diamond design even appears on the carpet.

393

Tomato-red plus sumptuous suede add up to an attention-grabbing piece of furniture. Indeed, a pair of these chairs is all that's needed to invigorate a room. Cocoa-brown suede welt helps define their graceful lines.

394

Think how uninspired this space would feel without the scarlet chenille chairs and door painted to match. The bright shades not only give the viewer a bit of a jolt (often a key component of modern decor), but also infuse the space with warmth and personality.

395

Be adventurous by choosing an unconventional color combination for a room. Here, turquoise blue, brown, and lime green give this bedroom a vivacious personality.

396

Floor-length draperies made from a striped tone-on-tone fabric harmonize with shimmery wall covering in a similar hue and reinforce the calming quality of a soft, monochromatic palette in a living room.

397

A vibrant red rug atop a faux marbleized wood floor helps ground the space in a two-story room. Tall curtains in the same hue as the carpet create visual unity and accentuate the scale.

398

Roll out a red carpet and you'll have enough character to keep everything else in the room neutral. Try contrasting the rich shade with an ethereal one that changes color with the light, such as the pale periwinkle seen here on the walls.

399

Pleated plaid chair covers may seem like an outlandish match for Chinoiserie furnishings, but the seats' fresh green shade and feminine style enable them to mingle effortlessly with the room's floral motifs.

400

•

One foolproof way to create a harmonious palette: work with shades that fall next to each other on the color wheel, such as the soft blues and mauves seen here.

401

•

Chairs featuring upholstery painted with elegant Chinoiserie scenes are a lovely counterpoint to modern accents, such as this squiggle-pattern rug and simple striped curtains.

402

Cover a set of dining chairs in several different colors of the same fabric for a subtle rainbow effect. Go with a simple pattern and muted hues to keep the look from appearing busy.

403

Cloud-white is a natural accent for linens, shades, and the like. To gaze up at this brilliant gathered canopy is almost like looking into a clear blue sky.

404

For those with color commitment issues, vibrant, patterned pillows, such as the ones in this teen's room, are an ideal solution. Less permanent than paint or upholstery, the cushions can be easily swapped in and out.

405

A built-in reading bench offers extra storage, with four drawers perfect for stowing photos, books, shoes, or whatever else can fit.

406

Give colorful pieces greater presence in a whitewashed space by "framing" them with both hard and soft edges. In this young girl's room, an iron daybed outlines a smattering of bright pillows, while a Lucite table subtly delineates a pair of graphic floor cushions.

FLORIDA KEYS
KEY WEST

407

You can't go wrong with a palette inspired by natural surroundings. In this beach house bedroom, blue-gray fabrics echo the shade of the sea on a stormy day and pale brown recalls the sand.

408

Fiery orange—a color the modernist Russian painter Wassily Kandinsky once compared to "a church bell, a strong contralto voice"—makes a powerful statement in any space. Temper it with a cool shade, such as blue, and notes of white.

409

A room composed of rose, pale lemon, and sky-blue shades has all of the energy a primary color palette imparts but none of the harshness. Mix in patterns for an even livelier look.

410

Gold accents bring sophistication to a bedroom, here by way of the handpainted chest of drawers and three-person bench at the foot of the bed.

411

The pictorial nature of toile makes it an ideal choice for a child's room. Opt for a modern, whimsical print like this red one, rather than a traditional style, which tends to be fancy.

412

Another fresh way to work with color is to choose pieces in different shades of one color. Here, a bed and chaise upholstered in pink velvet are accented with an antique rug and pillows in darker and lighter hues.

413

Some of the most striking contrasts come from juxtaposing pieces in complementary colors, such as the rosy carpet and emerald-green fronds in this sunroom. A smattering of neutral furnishings ensures that the combination isn't overpowering.

414

Create a segue between rooms by installing doorway curtains that set the tone for the space you're about to enter. Here, a pair of vibrant tartan panels hints at the grand yet cheerful sunroom beyond.

415

Here's an easy recipe for a dynamic color scheme: Choose a graphic abstract painting, then make sure each of its colors is represented at least once on a pillow, chair, vase, or another accent elsewhere in the room.

416

Punctuate a black-and-white palette—made more exciting here by layering different patterns—with pieces in a single bright hue, such as magenta, for a look that exudes modern glamour.

417

Beloved for its cheerful disposition, yellow can also look formal and sophisticated. If it's this muted glow (rather than a ray of sunlight) you're after, look no further than this elegant, golden tableau for inspiration.

418

An organic art glass panel is a beautiful vehicle for reinforcing a palette, such as the spring greens and neutrals seen here. If your taste is more traditional, opt for a less-abstract stained glass piece or perhaps a window salvaged from a church.

419

Let a two-color rug set the color palette for a room. In this living room, everything is a variation of red or light brown.

420

Modern abstract motifs often mimic the natural world, making them an ideal choice in a room with rustic accents. Notice, for example, how the shapes on this vivid rug subtly echo the stones on the fireplace.

421

One way to choose artwork for a neutral space: pick colors that are slightly brighter and have a bit more pigment than those already in the room. Here, straw yellow becomes a canary shade in the painting; tawny brown is translated as orange.

422

Hints of warm brass—on door handles, drawer pulls, candlesticks, and decorative nails—bring soft luster to a golden palette. To keep the metal gleaming, dust and clean occasionally with dish soap and warm water. Polish tarnished pieces when needed.

423

Some vases, like this ornate Imari pair, are colorful works of art. Let them shine by filling them with simple, unfussy flowers. Branches or foliage would also be a nice complement.

424

Classic blue-and-white dishware looks fresh when displayed not just in a china cabinet but also on walls, ledges, and sideboards. Here, the eclectic presentation suits the casual vibe of a rustic dining space.

425

Decoupage pieces—such as the colorful plates displayed here—can look surprisingly elegant, despite the humble materials (paper cutouts, varnish) used to create them.

426

Fresh flowers or fresh fruit can add a splash of color in a breakfast nook featuring neutral colors.

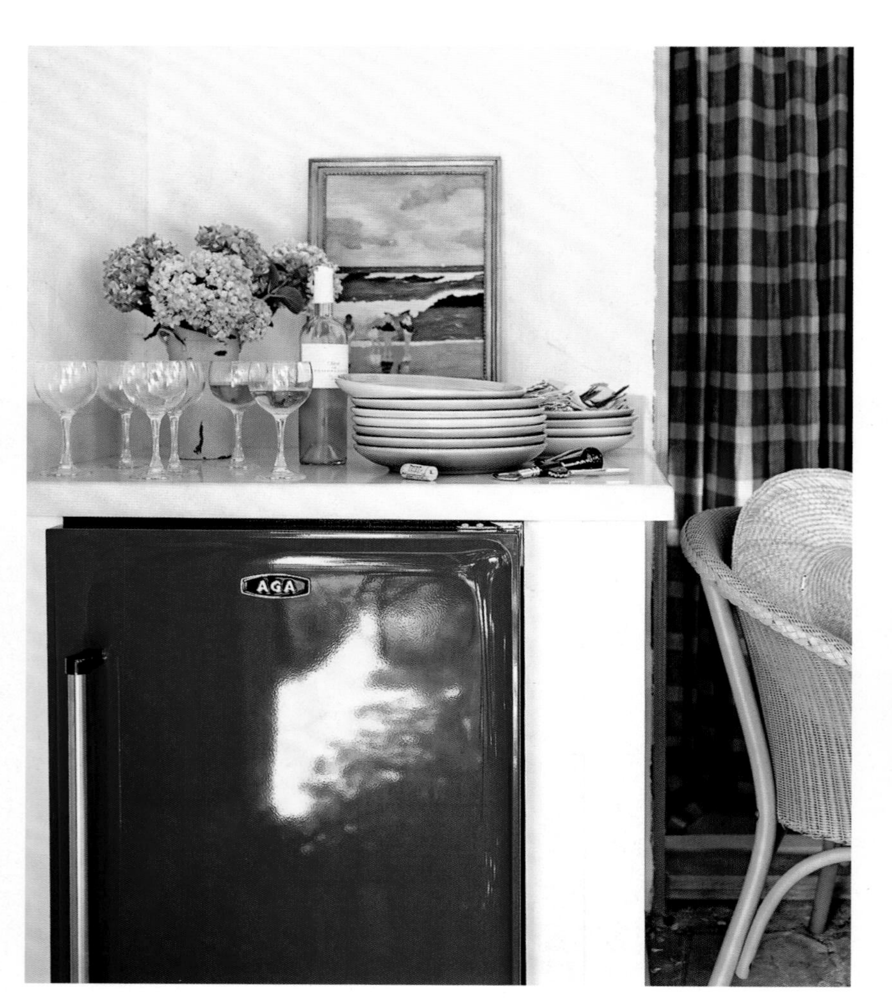
AGA

427

Small appliances—such as toasters, mixers, and beverage refrigerators like this one—now come in a rainbow of shades and offer a great opportunity to incorporate splashes of color into a kitchen.

428

For a chic party look, mix up a signature cocktail that tastes delicious *and* enhances the decor. This cranberry-guava drink, arranged on a lime-green tray, adds welcome bursts of bright color to a summertime fete.

429

Bring a whimsical touch to a snowy kitchen by painting stools in pretty pastel hues. Pinches of the same shades sprinkled throughout the room create a cohesive scheme.

430

Keep a red-and-green scheme from feeling one-note (or evocative of the holidays) by mixing patterns and integrating a wide range of shades, such as forest, lime, cherry, and cotton candy.

431

Bring extra cheer to the sunporch of a beach house by painting the walls and ceiling the same shade of sea green.

432

Keep an eclectic collection of wicker sunporch furniture from feeling too mismatched by using the same color palette for all of the cushions.

433

Brighten a collection of rattan furniture with a few coats of glossy spray paint. These items are upholstered with pieces cut from a vibrant, striped rug.

434

An outdoor space needn't be permanent. In this photo, an Indian wedding tent and some cast-off pillows define an appealing outdoor room. Commingling in a riot of color and patterns, the fabrics include everything from French country to Balinese designs.

435

Instead of planting a garden alongside a house, consider arranging pots of all shapes, colors, and sizes filled with lush blooms. The planters add texture and can be easily swapped in and out. For a coordinated look, choose flowers in variations on the same hue, such as pinks and oranges.

436

A lush blanket of ivy, which is hardy and easy to care for, brings glorious color to the facade of a house. Punctuate the emerald expanse with bright, contrasting shutters. Ivy is also a great solution for an unsightly wall.

437

Set against an alabaster backdrop, bright blue outdoor accents can magnify the brilliance of the sky. Together, the colors recall the whitewashed buildings topped with azure church domes that populate the Greek islands.

438

Faux bois furniture, made from a concrete-like resin shaped to look like twisted tree branches, can be a fitting accent in a garden. Update the style, which was invented in nineteenth-century France, with bright cushions.

439

Highlight a row of majestic-yet-unassuming trees, such as these scarlet oaks, with a shock of bright orange daylilies. The blooms require little maintenance beyond cutting them back in the fall.

440

A simple, unfinished red-wood arbor bordered by a tall hedge and dotted with an abundance of pink 'Zephrine Drouhin' roses creates a colorful entry to a garden.

Chapter 7 Quick Fixes

• 438 • • 441 • • 447 • • 452 • • 455 •

• 457 • • 460 • • 465 • • 468 • • 473 •

• 475 • • 481 • • 484 • • 487 • • 489 •

SO YOU'D LIKE to revitalize a room (or two) but not in the radical way often seen on television makeover shows. Let's just say you don't see yourself hiring a demolition crew, or even an interior designer, anytime soon. That's where the quick fix comes in—that relatively small but oh-so-satisfying upgrade you can do in a few days, a few hours, maybe even a few minutes. Whether it's applying a fresh coat of paint to the walls, replacing a window frame, finding the perfect spot for a flea market find, arranging potted plants around a doorway, or tying colorful cushions onto dark-colored chairs, you can easily put a new spin on a tired look. The change may not be dramatic, but you'll find the results gratifying nonetheless.

441

Enliven any space by painting the walls and ceiling two different hues, like the spicy paprika and saffron seen here.

442

It's amazing what a fresh coat of paint can do. Here, sky blue walls make white cotton chair covers, Murano glass chandeliers, and other furnishings seem brighter, their edges crisper.

443

●

Paint the back of a cabinet an electifying shade—such as the red shown here—and make a beautiful china service really pop. You can achieve a similar look with wallpaper.

444

For a touch of color in a neutral space, try painting just a window or doorframe, which is less expected (and less work) than painting an entire room. Note in this photo how the mint green breaks up the repetitiveness of the paneling in this kitchen.

445

Look for unconventional wall coverings. In this top-floor study, a map of the world was affixed like wallpaper to a canted wall. Framed maps on an adjoining wall echo the theme.

446

Instead of refinishing worn wood floors with polyurethane, consider painting them with bold stripes. The motif makes a room appear wider and grander, and can serve as a foundation for other patterns and colorful furnishings.

447

Mirrors—or in this case mirrored paneling in the fireplace and on a sconce—and whitewashed surfaces keep a cramped room with tiny windows from feeling too small or dark.

THE WEST
WILLIAM MORRIS
THE COLOURING, BRONZING AND PATINATION OF METALS
ALISON WEIR
THE CHILDREN OF HENRY VIII
SIMON SCHAMA
Industry & Design in the Netherlands 1850 1950
TWENTIETH-CENTURY ORNAMENT
BILLY BALDWIN decorates
DETAILS
KITCHENS
architectural fixtures and hardware
TEXTILES WIENER WERKSTÄTTE
American Porcelain 1770-1920
DUNBAR
THE OTHER BOLEYN GIRL
ORHAM SILVER

448

Try juxtaposing not just paint colors but finishes too. Here, white semigloss (the ideal finish for a bathroom) is used on the wainscoting and ceiling, while the rest of the walls are treated with soothing gray in a matte finish.

449

A sunroom with a ceiling covered in luminous silver leaf, a thin foil, positively glows. Purchase silver (or gold) leaf in rolls and apply it yourself, or hire a painter who specializes in decorative techniques to do the work. You can also get a similar effect with silver or gold paint.

THE HENRY CLAY FRICK HOUSES

450

If you entertain often, consider housing liquor and bar equipment in a beautiful armoire in the living room. A wall-mounted shelf can hold glasses. ◄

451

Refresh a tired or outdated sofa with new upholstery in a neutral color that won't go out of style, such as white. Change the look by rotating pillows with the seasons: pale cotton in summertime, dark-colored velvet in winter, and so on. ◄

452

Here's a simple way to customize a cushioned chair or stool: cover the top with a piece of canvas decorated with pretty grosgrain ribbon in varying widths and colors.

453

When painting furniture you use often, such as a dining table, choose a high-gloss product and top with several coats of a clear protective finish to guard against scratches, dings, and discoloration.

454

•

Revive flea-market chairs with white paint and fresh fabric, such as this vibrant Chinese print. You can do the upholstering yourself: just remove the seats, cut fabric to size, and affix with a staple gun.

455

An easy alternative to upholstering is to purchase seat cushions, which can instantly brighten dark chairs—like the vintage metal ones in this photo—or hide flaws on flea-market finds.

456

Eliminate clutter in a home office by storing everything from stationery to knitting needles in wicker baskets that can be easily tucked into bookshelves.

457

•

For a distinctive, pattern-on-pattern look, cover the back of a china cabinet with wallpaper that coordinates with, but doesn't match, that on the walls. The toile used here reinforces the room's red-and-white scheme and highlights a collection of antique dishes.

458

•

Here's an ingenious way to disguise a flat-screen TV. The custom-upholstered bench shown here has a detachable top. Remove the top and the screen pops up with the press of a button on a remote control.

robertRauschenberg.combines
malibu A Century of Living by the Sea

459

Transform beautiful found doors—here from Mexico—into decorative screens. Connect two or more panels with hinges and, if you like, replace panes with mirrors, as was done here. The pieces would also look pretty with their original glass.

460

Keep a small guest bedroom feeling airy and light by leaving canopy beds bare. Embellish them with small flourishes, such as the silver gilt finials seen here atop Colonial-style beds.

461

Give a garret guest bedroom a romantic air with a vintage metal-frame bed. In this room, the color of an old bench with chipped paint—placed at the foot of the bed—inspired the hues of lampshades, rugs, and blankets.

462

Create a dramatic, three-dimensional headboard in a snap by arranging a row of tall white shutters behind a bed. Use the same shutters on windows for a cohesive look.

463

Wicker furniture brings wonderful texture to casual decor. The pieces typically come in white or natural shades, but you can change them to any color you like with a few coats of glossy spray paint.

464

Define rooms—without closing them off completely—with a dramatic sweep of fabric drawn to one side. This striped silk curtain is mounted on a rod above an arched doorway and tied back with cord.

465

Convert a pair of pleated curtains into canopies for twin beds. To make them, two corbels were painted white and twenty-one eyehooks were screwed, evenly spaced, around their flat edges. The corbels were then mounted to the wall above the bed with heavy-duty picture hangers, graded for at least one hundred pounds. Curtain pins attached to each pleat were then hooked into the corbels' eyehooks.

466

Consider hanging tab-top curtains around the perimeter of a canopy bed. You can enshroud the bed entirely or install panels only at the back, creating a gauzy headboard.

467

Hang curtains outside a window seat. They can be pulled closed for privacy indoors.

468

●

Create a luxe, romantic look in a bedroom with curtains, bed hangings, a dust ruffle, and tablecloth that all graze or pool on the floor.

469

An antique kimono was used to create this extra-long bolster pillow, but you could create a similar effect with a beautiful piece of silk. Drape another swath of silk over a canopy bed or tie the fabric to the poles of a four-poster bed.

470

An Oriental rug, typically a living room mainstay, looks fresh in a bedroom. Even though these carpets are made of durable wool, you should vacuum them regularly to remove dirt that can break down the yarn fibers.

471

•

Bring softness and pattern to a bathroom vanity or sink area by replacing cabinet doors with a gathered fabric skirt. You could also dress up a freestanding vanity this way.

472

A vintage pull-work tablecloth is easy to transform into a charming shower curtain. Topstitched to the back of the tablecloth, a piece of lime-green fabric, with raw edges pressed in, provides a contrasting backing. Buttonholes along the top (made with a sewing machine) hold decorative hooks, which also support a plastic liner.

473

Customize a plain wreath to coordinate with your existing decor—in this case the ribbons on (and suspending) the wreath match the beige linen curtains lined with sage check fabric.

474

Give items displayed on shelves room to breathe so that you can truly enjoy each one. If you have a large collection and little space, rotate pieces in and out every so often.

KARL BLOSSFELDT
SCHIRMER/MOSEL

475

Canvases presented without frames have a three-dimensional effect. Set against a white background, the birds in these paintings appear to be in flight.

476

You may need to improvise a bit when hanging an odd number of prints, such as these nine vintage photographs. Here, the pictures are mounted not just above a credenza, but also over a chair; one print is dropped down to fill the gap between the furniture, creating a pleasing, balanced look.

477

•

A few pieces of Native American pottery bring rich color and intriguing forms to a small mantel. ◄◄

478

•

Add interest to a bare wall by mounting a vintage bracket upside down and using it to display a small collection—here of shells, sand dollars, and starfish. ◄

479

•

Spruce up a wall by gathering beautiful platters or other dishes at a flea market and then mounting them with plate hangers. Before hanging them, experiment with different configurations by making paper cutouts of the pieces and arranging them on the wall with painter's tape.

TKD

480

Easier than dividing one large map into framed sections (but just as spectacular), you can purchase a series of maps, frame them, and mount them en masse. This floor-to-ceiling display of sand-colored plats depicts Miami Beach in 1943.

481

Keep proportion in mind when playing with shapes in a room. Here, the generous size of a round mirror makes it work with an armless sofa's boxy silhouette. A circular table and trio of glass orbs echo the mirror's form.

482

Create a compelling tableau with a collection of similar artwork (here French landscapes) by hanging some items and propping up others in stands or against a wall.

483

A smattering of playful pieces—a fluorescent beach ball painting; bright, geometric-pattern vases; an oblong pendant lamp—keep the mood in a modern dining space light and fun.

484

One quirky piece, like this monkey-shape planter, and a lively yellow accent breathe new life into a contemporary kitchen—and reveal the owners' fun-loving sense of humor.

485

•

Considered a good-luck symbol, metal or wood barn stars—used to decorate barns in the eighteenth and nineteenth centuries—are often found at flea markets and antiques shops. The pieces have a cheerful, rustic quality that is just right for a kitchen.

CURRANTS
LOAF SUGAR
SUGAR
OAT MEAL
BARLEY
LOAF SUGAR
SUGAR
BUTTER

486

Sometimes a display can be both decorative and functional. Arranging a beautiful collection of dishes, such as this cheerful Cornish Ware, on open shelves is a great way to address both needs.

487

An American flag makes a strong statement indoors. This giant, vintage flag sets a bright color palette for a children's room.

488

Simple, practical items—a warm teak tray for holding toiletries, a pretty carved soap dish, an array of artful sea sponges—bring natural beauty to a bathroom.

489

Plants of all shapes and sizes—along with accessories such as floral pillows and a mirror frame crafted from twigs—help connect a screened-in porch to the outdoors.

490

Few color schemes pack more of a punch than black and white accented with a single vibrant hue, such as the coral seen on the patterned throw pillows in this breezy outdoor space.

491

When it comes to creating a sumptuous, inviting look, you can't have too many pillows. On this covered porch, pillows of all shapes and sizes in bright cottons and silks make a wrought-iron daybed an ideal spot to curl up for a nap.

492

Design a vibrant, semi-private outdoor shower stall by adding grommets to a pair of canvas panels, then threading ropes through and hanging the cloths from rods mounted overhead.

493

Let teak furniture weather naturally so that it effortlessly blends into its outdoor surroundings.

494

Beautiful containers, such as a handcrafted basket or vintage pot embellished with a mosaic, can make even familiar plants like petunias or marigolds feel distinctive.

495

Stationary sheer fabric panels soften sunlight without blocking views from a semi-enclosed outdoor space. They can be gathered with rope or twine for easy access to the surrounding gardens.

496

If you don't have room or time for a garden, you can still create a lush look by arranging planters around a doorway and letting vines like honeysuckle grow over a railing or fence.

497

Restore an old, chipped porch swing with a fresh coat of color: Scrape off loose paint and lightly sand. Prime, paint, and finish with a clear protective topcoat.

498

A swing made of fragrant, weather-resistant cedar, left in its natural color and finished with a clear stain, is extremely low maintenance. Dress it up with colorful pillows.

499

A brick house can be painted any color. A coat of pastel pink paint, tempered by warm gray shutters and white trim, gives the old-world material a dreamy, romantic air.

500

A teak table, seen here with Adirondack chairs that blend with the verdant landscape, is an ideal choice for an outdoor spot. The wood's high oil content makes it water- and rot-resistant so you can leave it out year round.

Chapter 8 Sophisticated Surroundings

• 495 •
• 498 •
• 502 •
• 505 •
• 508 •
• 513 •
• 515 •
• 526 •
• 534 •
• 539 •
• 541 •
• 551 •
• 558 •
• 560 •
• 570 •

SOPHISTICATED SURROUNDINGS are for those who cherish the finest things in life. They are likely to be found in a formal home, inspired by stately English manors, sophisticated French châteaus, or elegant Italian palazzi. Their structure and form may be rooted firmly in the past, yet with interiors that are likely to include a refreshing mix of European or American antiques and fine art along with contemporary colors, creature comforts, and amenities. Public rooms are distinctly defined for specific purposes—formal and casual dining, reading, entertaining—while private rooms are the embodiment of luxury. Manicured gardens and grounds might include clipped parterres, a pergola or gazebo, and perhaps a garden folly, such as wedding-cake topiary.

501

Place a skirted round table in one part of a large living room and surround it with upholstered benches to define a distinct seating zone for reading or taking tea.

502

Refresh a traditional room that has a grand scale by keenly editing furnishings and restricting patterns to pillows and other decorative accents.

503

Cover the walls of a living room with custom-designed, hand-painted silk wallpaper and let it set the color scheme for the room.

504

Hang an unframed painting in an entrance hall to fill a large empty wall and provide an elegant greeting for guests.

505

•

Bring a seasonal note to a cheerful window seat on a stair landing by filling a tall vase with flowering branches.

VRBINO

506

•

Allow antique furnishings and accents to stand out by limiting the palette of fabrics to creams and whites and setting them off with surfaces of stone and wood.

507

•

Hang a large painting above a staircase to create high visual impact.

508

•

Hang a Japanese screen over a Regency settee in an entrance hall to create a warm, rich, and striking effect.

509

Keep an expansive living room vibrant by mixing styles of furniture and collectibles, all in the same color palette to maintain a sense of unity.

510

•

Have the floor of an entry hall hand-painted with faux marquetry that matches the style of not only the hall but also the adjoining living room.

511

•

Shake up a Louis XVI canapé with bold stripes and leopard pillows that add a playful sophistication to the traditional antique.

512

Update the dark vestibule of an urban maisonette with a minimalist contemporary painting mounted above an intricately carved console.

513

●

Enrich a Louis XV settee with a trim in a contrasting color. Complement the richness of the ceiling-to-floor drapes with patterned cushions on the sofa.

514

●

Cover the floor with a wool carpet woven on an old loom in a subtle custom pattern. Choose a neutral color for versatility.

515

Use contrasting wall treatments in adjoining rooms. Shown here is a foyer with Chinese-themed wallpaper, while the living room displays antique British and American portraits.

516

Apply a custom glaze to the walls and mount a Regency-style mirror above an elegant mantel.

517

Cover the living room floor with a highly-patterned carpet and pick up its color palette in the walls, drapes, and furniture.

518

Restore the entrance of an old house to its former glory with period details and artisanal touches like handcrafted woodwork and antique tapestry.

519

Install a pair of chandeliers to reflect antique silver-and-gold tea-chest paper on the cathedral ceiling of a tall entrance hall.

520

Embellish a coffered ceiling with delicate stencil work and employ a densely fringed, oversized ottoman as a coffee table.

521

Pep up and modernize a collection of traditional living room furnishings with leopard-print accents.

522

Top the mantel in a drawing room with an ornate mirror (here, in the 18th-century Irish Gothic style) and cover the walls with a complementary wallpaper.

523

Display and protect a collection of antique blue-and-white porcelain in a corner hutch in the dining room of a weekend house.

524

Cover the walls with hand-painted wallpaper that echoes the floral patterns and color palettes of antique ceramic jars.

525

Instead of using wallpaper, cover the walls of a dining room with a large collection of antique prints.

526

Place an arrangement of *Lysimachia ciliata* 'Purpurea,' magnolia seed pods, and skimmia berries in a silver footed urn on a sideboard.

527

Place a distinctive item of interest in the room—here a French terra-cotta wall fountain complemented by Regency-style chairs upholstered in a bold pattern.

528

Bring a formal touch to a dining table in a country house by topping it with a pristine vintage tablecloth and setting it with fine china.

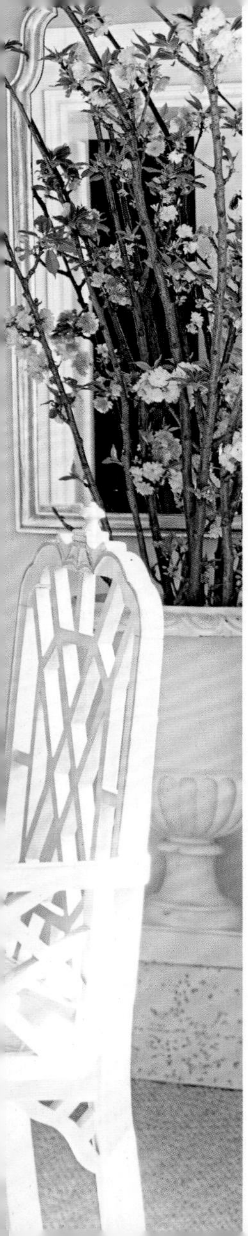

529

Enliven a dining room table with a pair of Chippendale-style chairs and cover the others in a mix of onyx leather and damask in a vivid hue.

530

Add an elegant note to a breakfast nook in a country house by slipcovering chairs in toile fabric and adding crisp trim at the edge of the skirts.

531

Commission a mural for the walls and include a round Regency mahogany table and chairs with quatrefoil backs and turquoise leather seat cushions.

532

Treat the walls of a formal dining room to multiple coats of brown lacquer for a rich and lustrous effect.

533

Instead of one long rectangular table, choose two smaller round tables to give a formal dining room a fresh twist that promotes intimate conversations.

534

•

Cover the walls of a dining room with a floral wallpaper and fill a large urn with flowering branches that echo the theme.

535

For a black-tie New Year's Eve dinner, tuck a monogram into tiny silver-plate frames for guests at each place setting.

536

Follow the 19th-century custom of including a smaller, skirted luncheon table in the same room as the main dining table.

537

Have a custom hood installed over a large, professional cooking suite topped with stainless steel counters.

538

Create a dramatic focal point in a kitchen by integrating a Tuscan-inspired hearth and placing a pair of white loggia chairs in front of it.

539

•

Add color and texture to a light, monochromatic kitchen with an interesting flooring—such as the red and beige checked floors here.

540

•

Build a butler's pantry with a swinging door next to the kitchen and enhance the cabinet doors with handsome bullet hinges. Here, the counters are topped with Calacatta Gold marble.

541

Fill a tall pot with ease right on the stove by installing an adjustable pivoting faucet behind the cooktop.

542

•

Fill the shelves of a library with art books and display a collection of prints with identical matting and frames.

543

•

Place a plaster bust on a heavily carved writing table to create a classical look echoed in an ornate mirror over the mantle.

544

•

Set a warm, welcoming tone in a sitting room with a fabulous Chinese rug and modern wingback chairs flanking the fireplace.

545

•

Mount extendable brass lamps that hang over built-in bookshelves to aid in finding books in the evenings.

546

Hang engravings (here a series of 17th- and 18th-century Dutch works) above a fireplace to add an historical element to a music room or study.

547

Include a pair of antique Regency chairs in a library and brighten the windows with Roman shades made with a lively fabric that still lets light through.

548

Give a library with Tudoresque windows a theatrical quality using intensely colored walls and draperies trimmed with extra-long fringe.

549

The angle of the sun changes the nature of color—such as a deep red on the walls—so be sure to take location into account when choosing a color scheme.

550

Add zest to a library by upholstering furniture in bright red-and-white crewel fabric and covering the floor with an ocelot-patterned carpet.

551

•

An ornate feature—such as this 17th-century Baroque fireplace—requires bold companions, such as a dramatic rug and boldly detailing ceiling.

552

•

Choose a palette for a room starting with a painting or carpet you plan to use in it.

553

●

For a heady glamour in a living room, include a mix of treasures like a screen, a large piece of branching coral, a zebra-skin rug, and a chaise longue.

554

Mount a freewheeling yet symmetrical arrangement of pictures above an overstuffed sofa covered in chintz and topped with plenty of pillows.

555

Separate public from private rooms with a padded door covered in baize and monogrammed with French nails.

556

•

Maximize the height and elegance of a dressing room by lining both sides of the space with carefully proportioned wardrobes.

557

Mount an embroidered hanging from India on the wall behind a mirrored four-poster bed, and complement the hanging with a large rug in the same color palette.

Rita Rudner Naked Beneath My Clothes
Joseph Wambaugh
Bogart
Eric Lax

558

Top a bed with a sumptuous canopy that features the same design as the wallpaper, upholstered headboard, pillow shams, and even an eye mask.

559

Enrich the walls of a master suite with a pattern of subtle stripes. Echo the wall color in the upholstered headboard and canopy fabric.

560

Give a luxurious guest room French country charm with downy toile bed linens and an upholstered headboard.

561

Top the barley-twist bedposts of an ebonized bed with a blue velvet bed valence trimmed with gold braid and curtains that can be pulled open and closed.

562

Enrich a vaulted ceiling of the sitting area of a master bedroom with hand-painted scenery and an elegantly understated chandelier.

563

•

Add style and function to a little girl's room with built-in clothing armoires whose windows are lined with pale pink fabric panels.

564

Use one pattern in a small boy's room for the wallpaper, upholstered headboard, bed skirt, and draperies. Top the bed with simple linens to provide a visual break from the pattern.

565

Place a seat, here a gilded-and-lacquered Hepplewhite bench, at the foot of a canopied four-poster bed in a room where pink is anything but frivolous.

566

•

Give character to a guest room with draperies and bed hangings made from antique toile that complements a delightful hand-painted antique chest used as a side table.

567

Position a linen-velvet upholstered wing chair next to an antique-style tub to bring a sense of comfort to an expansive bathroom.

568

Install caramel-colored onyx on the floor, counters, tub deck, and shower walls of a master bath.

569

Create an air of 1930s glamour in a bathroom with mirrored walls and doors and a sumptuous vintage-style tub.

570

Feel free, in an oversize bathroom to place an ornate side chair, antique plant stand, and Oriental rug.

571

Include potted orange trees or aspidistra plants to add greenery to a long, narrow colonnaded second-floor gallery.

572

Top a *faux bois* table on a porch with a candelabrum and handblown wine glasses for a late-summer brunch.

573

Frame a view into a sunroom with a fresh-hued tartan fabric portiere and cover the windows with lace shades. ▶

574

Complement floral patterns in a sunroom with fresh flowers and flowering plants. ▶

575

In a private garden surrounded by a tall brick wall, create an Edenesque lawn with ribbons of box-framed parterres.

576

Give a large expanse of lawn a more pleasing scale and proportion by defining it with beds in a pattern along the sides.

577

Install a stone fountain as an elegant focal point in the center of a formal garden surrounded by mature trees.

578

Add texture to an elaborate garden with a stone wall assembled in a way that makes it look natural to its surroundings.

579

Curve garden edges along or around the lawn for a more organic, less cultivated look.

580

•

In the realm of fantasy: If you've got acres and acres and love wine, grow your own grapes.

581

•

Separate a terrace from the lawn with a semicircular bed surrounding a small pool and fountain, and add color to the house with climbing bougainvillea.

582

•

Make use of a hillside by turning it into a multilevel garden with sharply angled hedges and curved plants and a path of stepping stones.

583

Soften the geometry of the clipped hedges and obelisks of a formal French-style garden with flowers in a limited palette, such as white cosmos, purple salvia, and yellow rudbeckia.

584

Enrich a formal garden with a luminescent quality at dusk by planting white flowering plants and trees, such as 'Natchez' crepe myrtle, camellias, oak-leaf hydrangeas, magnolias, impatiens, azaleas, Mexican plum, and caladiums.

585

Encircle a painted terra-cotta urn with Asian jasmine in a garden for a heavenly scent.

586

Plant creeping fig to cover a brick wall enclosing a formal garden and trim it twice a week in summer.

Virgo

Chapter 9 Eclectic Environment

• 576 •

• 580 •

• 586 •

• 588 •

• 592 •

• 595 •

• 600 •

• 603 •

• 607 •

• 614 •

• 616 •

• 619 •

• 621 •

• 625 •

• 630 •

THE ECLECTIC ENVIRONMENT is home to the worldly adventurer. Artfully peppered with an exotic mix of furnishings and artifacts from faraway places, its living spaces may house a lantern from Morocco, a coffee table from India, and colorful silk cushions from Thailand. These spaces may just as well include a commingling of modern art and antique furniture, or contemporary furniture and primitive accents from Africa or South America. Talismans from around the globe—a pre-Columbian figurine, perhaps, or a 19th-century Chinese Buddha—infuse private spaces with energy and individuality. Outside, a Chinese lantern might illuminate a Tahitian teak table surrounded by Portuguese chairs.

The only constant in such homes is the element of surprise.

587

Create a modern fusion look in a sitting room with a mix of Asian, contemporary, and European furnishings in a monochromatic palette.

588

•

For an unusual display, mount a door—here an 18th-century carved wooden one from the Piedmont region of Italy—on the wall of a high-ceilinged living room.

589

•

Evoke a masculine atmosphere in a drawing room by mixing hand-wrought elements from different places and periods, such as a rusted metal chandelier, an antique carved statue of a saint, and 18th-century armchairs.

590

●

Mix antiques, such as this William IV rosewood table, with modern art, such as this photograph by Valerie Belin, to give fresh energy to a living room.

591

●

Lacquer the walls of a room with white high-gloss paint to allow an array of multicultural furnishings from different eras to stand out in relief.

592

Enliven a traditional room paneled in mahogany by painting the ceiling with a geometric pattern and adding mid-20th-century furnishings from Italy, France, and America. The result: a timeless look.

593

Cover pillows on a sofa with variegated Indian silks that add pattern to a largely patternless room.

594

Blend a mix of antique furnishings from different eras and places, such as this 19th-century Italian gilt mirror, 18th-century apothecary jars, and a 17th-century English hall chair, to add interest to a living room.

VOYAGES
THE QUEST FOR PARADISE

595

Set off contemporary furniture with a mix of antiques, mid-20th-century pieces, a fanciful crystal chandelier, and a faux-skin rug.

596

Brighten a dark, moody entrance hall of a Tudor structure by gray-washing the architectural timbers, painting the floor with an appealing geometric pattern, and placing potted topiaries in rush baskets for a modern sensibility.

597

Enrich a great room with a mix of periods and styles—here, Louis XV chairs, a teak table from Thailand, and a shepherd's chest from Greece.

598

Cover the living room floor with a dramatic rug and dress the windows with draperies made of a heavy and striking fabric. ▸

599

Refresh traditional pieces with a surprising upholstery fabric and trim treatment. ▸

MANHATTAN

600

Create a little tension in a living room by mixing something modern, like a painting by Yayoi Kusama, with something baroque, such as an antique French chandelier.

601

Upholster a pair of formal chairs with raffia and white canvas, and place them on either side of a large armoire.

602

Install a creamy carpet with a nail-head trim in the anteroom of a living space and have the walls painted with a chinoiserie mural.

603

Give a family room energy with a worldly mix of furnishings, such as a pair of Brighton Pavilion–inspired tortoise-shell bamboo chairs, a polished dark-wood African stool, and some contemporary X benches covered in deer skin.

604

Bring a spicy note to a dining room by loosely hanging a boldly patterned antique Indian appliquéd textile on one wall.

605

Add an untraditional touch to a dining room by placing an unexpected lighting fixture—a floor lamp—next to the table.

606

Slipcover dining chairs with peppy Indian cotton stripes and hang a graphic white plaster-of-Paris candle chandelier over the middle of the table.

607

Hang a tapestry in a formal and high-ceilinged dining room.

608

Mix up the styles in a rustic barn-themed room by adding modern touches—such as the industrial lighting fixture over the table or contemporary vases and a glass centerpiece.

609

Bring an unconventional touch to the dining area of a ranch house by upholstering chairs in pink-and-peach Fortuny fabric. ◄

610

Juxtapose a dark carved refectory table with a modern pendant light fixture and an abstract painting.

611

Create a dining room table center-piece from ostrich eggs and bone accessories.

612

●

Carve out a charming breakfast nook by placing a round table in front of an upholstered bench and pulling up a couple of mismatched stools.

613

●

Add texture to the wall of a small dining area with a trellis-like design behind an overstuffed banquette. ▶

614

•

Add an unexpected modern element—such as this Lichtenstein print above the fireplace—to an otherwise traditional dining room.

615

Use antique tiles on the floor and backsplash of a rustic kitchen and surround a central table with contemporary chairs.

616

•

Commission an artisan to craft a pair of freestanding cabinets and have them painted a lively color, such as golden chartreuse, and then distressed for an aged look.

617

Hand-paint the names of French desserts on tin storage bins stashed in the open shelves of a kitchen island.

618

Add a touch of whimsy to a kitchen by hanging a delicate chandelier over an island.

619

Display a collection in an elegant wooden dresser. Here are French handblown antique bottles and contemporary salad plates in an 18th-century Alsatian hutch.

620

Mix modern elements, such as Knoll bar stools or a classic George Nelson pendant, with Arts and Crafts–style cabinets in a kitchen.

621

Furnish a study with an artful mélange of pieces, such as an Oriental rug, alabaster table lamps, Roman end tables, and a Swedish coffee table. (The one shown here is made from rosewood, zebrawood, and ebonized birch.)

622

Add interest and function to a gallery leading to a study by incorporating a Chinese altar table for stacks of books and collectibles.

623

•

Add color and shimmer to a Middle-Eastern–inspired reading nook with lots of colorful silk-covered pillows and silk-upholstered walls.

XLIX
HERBARIUM
TREMOLS
XLVIII
HERBARIUM
TREMOLS
VANITY FAIR'S HOLLYWOOD
oceanic art

624

Give a reading room in a ranch house an air of bohemian luxury by covering the floor with an Oriental rug and placing assorted chinoiserie pieces on shelves.

625

Cover one wall with an assemblage of offbeat works of art, including paintings, drawings, masks, and other collected items to give a home office unconventional flair.

ITALIAN SPLENDOR
FULL MOON
Jerusalem and the Holy Land Rediscovered
The Prints of David Roberts (1796–1864)
LONDON ARCHITECTURE
MEGALITHS
PAUL CAPONIGRO
LIFE
magnum
WITHOUT SANCTUARY
LONDON
THE EARTH FROM THE AIR
Spain
ROME
DEAN KOONTZ
Salman Rushdie
Sicily
TRAFFIC AND LAUGHTER
KATE'S HOUSE
AMY TAN
JOYCE CAROL OATES
THE KITCHEN GOD'S WIFE
PHILIP LARKIN

626

Use unusual decorative textiles for window treatments. Here an antique *suzani* is used for a Roman shade.

627

Brighten up a study or den by painting built-in bookshelves a vibrant yellow or other cheerful color.

628

Give a guest room personality by making a gorgeous iron bed the focal point. Shown here is a 17th-century Tuscan bed.

629

●

Place a trunk or sailor's chest at the foot of a bed in a beachside vacation home. The one shown here comes from Greece and was hand-painted.

630

Place a provincial 18th-century Italian table on wheels between a pair of Colonial-style twin beds in a guest room.

631

Display a one-of-a-kind collection—shown here are carved *santos* and religious artifacts—on a ledge above the bed in a guest room.

632

Evoke a Russian dacha in the guest room of an American cabin with a canopied bed, an antler mirror, and a painted chest of drawers.

633

Add personality to a bedroom with a dramatic decoupaged chest topped with a simple mirror, small painting, elaborate lamp, and unique sculpture.

634

Display treasures from your travels. Shown here is an 18th-century Thai monk's bench used as a night table, topped with a pair of Burmese teardrop mirrors and a contemporary lamp.

Virgo
james rosenquist
ahead of the 21st century

635

•

Cover a plain bed with a dramatic bedspread or quilt to add color and to make up, visually, for the lack of a headboard. Shown here is an antique pink and green *suzani*.

636

In a master bedroom, add character by topping a bench at the foot of the bed with a kilim rug.

637

Add character to a small powder room by hanging a custom-framed mirror assembled from pieces of antiqued mirror and rosettes.

638

Leave the door of a medicine cabinet open to display a visually interesting collection of glass bottles, canisters, and other toiletry containers.

639

Add drama and texture to a small bathroom by covering the walls with large, dark blue tiles.

640

Break from the usual and opt for tall matching lamps on a bathroom counter with two sinks, instead of mounted wall lighting.

641

Add a mirrored armoire in a large bathroom to ensure abundant storage space and provide the convenience of a full-length mirror.

642

Create an antique-country atmosphere in a bathroom by covering the top portion of the walls with wide horizontal natural-wood planks and the lower portion with white beadboard.

643

Create a place for contemplation on a covered loggia by pairing a British Colonial chaise with an Asian stool, which can serve as a perch for a glass of wine and a book.

644

Add zest to a poolroom with a boldly striped wraparound sofa, red leather ottoman, and Moroccan-themed accents.

645

Add warmth to a sunroom by installing a fireplace and flanking it with a pair of painted rattan chaise longues that have thick cushions for extra comfort.

646

Add a playful note to an ocean-front gazebo by painting a Matisse-inspired frieze of frolicking swimmers near the ceiling.

647

In keeping with the Creole tradition, paint the French doors of a *garçonnière* a bright coral color to lend punch to a courtyard and ensure a cheerful welcome upon arrival.

648

Bring an exotic look to a labyrinth garden by installing a Japanese-style bridge and planting red Japanese maple trees.

649

Scatter columns of various heights and styles throughout a garden to get an eclectic look.

650

•

If your property is naturalistic and informal, consider adding a fieldstone-lined brook as a refreshing and casual water feature.

Chapter 10 Serene Retreat

• 635 •

• 636 •

• 643 •

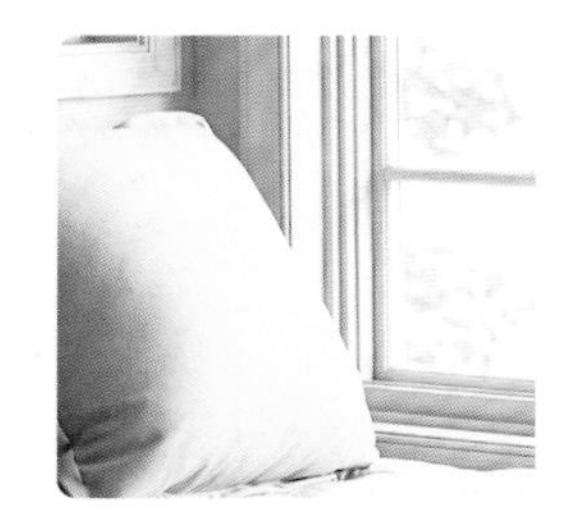

• 650 •

• 652 •

• 653 •

• 656 •

• 661 •

• 665 •

• 667 •

• 671 •

• 675 •

• 681 •

• 685 •

• 689 •

THE SERENE RETREAT provides an oasis of comfort and calm for those who regard their home as a sanctuary. Imbued with quiet, neutral palettes, natural fabrics, and a minimalist mix of comfortable furnishings, the gathering spaces in these dwellings are as soothing to the senses as the private rooms. Subtle textures and patterns appeal to the eye; the sound of a trickling fountain provides a balm to frayed nerves; and candles, rosemary topiaries, or fresh flowers fill the air with a crisp, clean scent. The light from a single hurricane lamp might illuminate a covered terrace at night, or a Zenlike pool house might punctuate a view across a placid pool.

651

•

Lighten up a traditional living room by adding new pieces with unfussy lines and white slipcovers or upholstery.

652

•

Install monochromatic floor-to-ceiling draperies to add softness to a formal living room.

653

Frame individual pieces of an antique map of a European city, such as Paris, and mount them on a wall in a living room to create an evocative yet tranquil backdrop.

654

As a foil for a serene room, include richly textured upholstery and unexpected touches, such as this modern lamp.

655

A high-backed sofa will lend intimacy to an expansive living room and makes a great spot for a nap as it envelopes you like a cocoon.

THE SERENGETI'S
GREAT MIGRATION

656

Place an extra-large leather upholstered ottoman between a pair of sofas and a couple of chairs upholstered in muted dusty hues of linen, such as gray-blue or taupe.

657

Create a restful ambience in a living room with fabrics and furnishings in an easy-on-the-eye palette of cream, beige, taupe, and pale blue.

658

Paint the walls of a family room a soothing shade of pale green and keep fabric patterns subtle to cultivate relaxation and comfort.

659

Wash a living room in caramel, biscuit, and cream tones, and include subtly textured rugs to create a soothing atmosphere.

660

Create a sense of calm around one striking feature in a room by keeping the surrounding décor muted in comparison. The stark walls and select few decorative pieces in this entrance hall offset the drama of a grand, curving staircase.

661

Objects don't have to be placed symmetrically on a mantel—a lone candlestick, carved box, or interesting vase can provide a perfect finishing touch.

662

Hang a large, contemporary black-and-white photograph over a sofa in the living room of a small urban apartment.

663

Set off sofas and chairs covered in white cotton duck with dark antique wood furnishings in a high-ceilinged living room.

Andy Goldsworthy WALL
ANNIE LEIBOVITZ WOMEN SUSAN SONTAG

664

Let the creams, browns, silvers, and grays of an antique Kirman rug inspire the palette for the furnishings, fabrics, and finishes in a living room.

665

Create an intimate gathering space by angling four wing-back chairs around a starkly modern fireplace.

666

Carve out a private niche in a family room by placing a thickly cushioned window seat—with a reading lamp mounted on the wall—in a remote corner.

667

Orient a long dining table toward oversized picture windows overlooking a view of a natural body of water or soothing landscape.

668

Inject a touch of sparkle in a minimalist dining space with a 1960s gold-plated crystal chandelier.

669

Warm up an ultramodern dining space with a macadamia-colored calfskin floor covering and some high-backed armchairs upholstered in pale pistachio linen.

670

Create an all-white backdrop in a dining room and surround the table with comfortable leather chairs.

671

Top a banquette with a thick cushion and lots of silk pillows for extra seating in a dining room.

672

Set up a charming dining spot in a windowed corner of a kitchen with a pair of antique barstools and a tall bistro table.

673

Surround a round walnut table in a formal dining room with tufted chairs covered in plush mohair velvet.

674

Establish a soothing ambience with furnishings and finishes in a mix of materials, such as a wrought-iron chandelier, a table made of antique oak, and bluestone flooring.

675

Visually separate a kitchen from an adjoining room or a busy stairwell with a Mondrianesque fiberglass screen that shields the view but still admits light.

676

Paint cabinetry in a country kitchen with stainless-steel appliances a restful, neutral color.

677

Forego window treatments in a kitchen to let in natural light and paint the walls varying shades of the subtlest greens.

678

•

Establish a sense of ease and order in the kitchen by positioning a pull-out pantry next to the refrigerator.

679

•

Install a small sink in a marble-topped kitchen island for convenience while prepping food.

680

Incorporate a wine refrigerator and microwave into the cabinetry so that they blend into the style and decor of the kitchen.

681

Create a sense of balance and harmony in a kitchen by contrasting white or cream-colored cabinetry with dark-wood barstools, cocoa-colored window shades, or a customized copper range hood.

682

Hide books in a library on shelves behind paneled doors, where they will still be easily accessible.

683

Juxtapose pieces of different periods but with the same level of detail to project a balanced yet eclectic style.

684

•

Upholster a pair of wing chairs in a den with a subtle tweed in an oatmeal color. ◄

685

•

Top a mantel with a striking bronze bust or contemporary sculpture to create a focal point in a den. ◄

686

•

Take advantage of a magnificent view—here, a sleek glass-topped desk is positioned against a wall of windows overlooking the ocean.

687

Include a writing desk and comfortable chair for letter writing in a master bedroom.

688

Eschew bright colors in a child's room, opting instead for a sophisticated mix of creams, tans, and taupes, spiced with accents in mustard, chili pepper, or saffron hues.

689

Install a fireplace in a large master bedroom and surround it with chairs or a sofa upholstered in fabrics with subtle patterns or pale solid colors.

690

Hang a large square mirror over a mantel to brighten and open up an already serene sitting room.

691

•

Include a slipcovered chaise longue near a bay window in a bedroom to create a comfortable spot for reading, napping, or just gazing out the window.

692

Include accents in washed-out natural hues to promote a peaceful atmosphere conducive to restful sleep in a master bedroom.

693

Commission the design of a continuous headboard that runs wall to wall and cover it with 100-percent linen in a flax color.

694

Establish a soothing quality in a bedroom by pairing neutral tones and natural fabrics with dreamy, smoky mirrors that catch sunlight from a nearby window.

695

Use a bamboo shade as the backdrop to a sitting area composed of two overstuffed chairs sharing a small ottoman in a master bedroom.

696

Decorate a master bedroom in soothing shades of caramel, brown, and ivory, and tuck the bed within a creamy millwork alcove.

697

Hang a mosquito net over the bed of a guest room in a tropical vacation house and cover the bed with white antique French linens.

698

Paint the walls of a bedroom a pale gray-blue and base the color palette of the accents and furnishings in the room on that hue.

699

Surround a poster bed with a minimalist canopy that can be pulled open and closed on both sides.

700

Cover doors that open onto a balcony or terrace with tall, slim shutters that can be opened to let in breezes.

701

Combine brick-shaped tile with Carrara marble for a modern spa-like quality in a bathroom featuring dark wood and twin sinks.

702

●

Cultivate a sense of harmony and balance in a master bath by placing twin vanities—built like furniture—to face each other across the room.

703

Create serenity in a bathroom by placing a sculptural tub in front of a floor-to-ceiling window overlooking a water view.

704

Construct a symmetrical pavilion for outdoor relaxing or entertaining at the far end of a pool. Install a fireplace for warmth on chilly evenings.

705

Add luminosity to a sunroom by painting the ceiling with silver leaf and installing shutters to control the amount of light let in.

706

Set a fireplace into the limestone wall of an outdoor pavilion and surround it with a mix of comfortable furniture upholstered in a creamy cotton duck.

707

Use a large coffee table as the centerpiece of a porch and as a place to display books and other collectibles.

708

Consider redoing a piece of sunroom furniture with an unexpected choice of paint or fabric—such as staining a wicker chair dark mahogany and upholstering cushions in chenille or luxurious suede—to let you see it in a whole new way.

709

Enhance the splendor of a view of wooded hills by planting a low hedge of *Berberi's thunbergii* 'Crimson Pygmy' instead of beds of flowers, and—if your budget allows—incorporate a massive abstract sculpture.

710

Line a long gravel driveway with an abundance of lavender to create a heavenly scented welcome or farewell.

711

Give a large expanse of lawn a naturally artful focal point by planting a character-filled specimen tree, such as Japanese maple.

Chapter 11 Comfortable Haven

• 696 •

• 698 •

• 704 •

• 709 •

• 711 •

• 716 •

• 719 •

• 725 •

• 727 •

• 729 •

• 730 •

• 735 •

• 739 •

• 740 •

• 747 •

THE COMFORTABLE HAVEN puts no-frills, no-fuss people at ease. Durable flooring, wash-and-wear cotton duck slipcovers, and lots of fluffy pillows and soft throws are de rigueur in its living and family rooms, and hard-to-stain countertops and easy-to-clean cabinets are standard in its kitchen. Storage spaces—from bookshelves with louvered doors to window seats with pull-out drawers—abound in every room, keeping the whole house free of clutter. Simple Roman shades add privacy and control light in bedrooms and baths. And informal pathways lead children from the house to the playhouse, while low-fuss plants keep yardwork to a minimum.

712

Furnish the corner of a large living room with a sectional sofa, its thick cushions and plentiful pillows offering extra comfort.

713

Create a relaxed ambience in the living room/sunporch of a summer house with vintage American wicker furniture enameled chocolate brown.

714

Provide low-cost comfortable seating for children in a family room by placing large, square floor cushions around a coffee table.

715

Give a living room a casual atmosphere with floor coverings made from a natural material, like coir or jute, in natural colors.

716

In lieu of a small, delicate cocktail table, choose a pair of chenille-covered square ottomans, which can serve as small tables, extra seating, or a place to put up your feet.

717

For a clean, easy-to-maintain, and minimalist look, paint a basic brick fireplace with white high-gloss paint.

718

Keep a collection of books dust-free but still accessible in a tall cabinet with glass doors placed beside the fireplace.

719

Warm up the wood floors of a casual living room with a flat-weave rug in a neutral color.

720

Add variety to a symmetrically arranged living room with a mixture of round, square, and rectangular pillows, and with non-matching side tables.

721

•

Free up a lot of space in a small family room by hanging a flat-screen television on the wall and eliminating a bulky console.

722

Keep the family room calm—no matter how busy the activities get—by using comforting and neutral tones.

723

Create a streamlined yet luxurious dining room by surrounding a sculptural monolithic dining table with chairs upholstered in leather, covering the ceiling with pewter-leaf tea paper, and installing an Art Deco iron-and-glass chandelier.

724

Carve out a breakfast area in a kitchen with four painted-wood folding chairs around a flea-market farm table placed by a window.

725

In a dining area next to a wall of windows, create a sense of being outdoors with a sleek wood table and director's chairs with child-friendly leather seats.

726

Allow for an easy-to-host brunch for twelve by including an extendable Parsons table with a lacquered bar-top finish in a breakfast room.

727

To keep a room from getting locked into one time period, layer it with an array of styles, such as a set of 1960s pendant lighting fixtures over a French country farm table.

728

Use simple, white subway tiles in a kitchen for an easy-to-clean backsplash and clean, minimalist look.

729

Paint kitchen cabinets the same pale yellow used on the walls to promote a sense of harmony in a country kitchen.

730

Warm up a big kitchen and adjoining family room with old-fashioned beadboard on the walls and ceiling.

731

Combine recessed and pendant lights on the ceiling to offer the choice of bright or atmospheric lighting.

732

•

Top counters with Formica edged with stainless steel and cover the high-traffic area of floor in front of the sink with a coir runner or rug.

733

•

Doorless shelves under the kitchen counter allow easy access to pots and pans.

734

Use honed semi-polished bluestone for countertops and backsplashes—it's practical and stain-resistant.

735

Display an eclectic and multi-hued collection of plates, teapots, and bowls on open shelves surrounding a kitchen sink.

Wine
WINE

736

Craft an eating ledge made of Corian around a food prep island so that the cook can have company while preparing meals.

737

Install open shelves over a sink in a country kitchen for a pretty display and to keep kitchen items within reach.

738

Carve out a small work area with a desk, a laptop, and some drawers or shelves and mount a mirror television nearby to increase the function of a kitchen.

739

•

Construct a plate rack over the sink for easy access. And install deep drawers on either side of the sink for storage of pots and pans and other kitchenware.

740

•

The top ledge of cream-colored kitchen cabinets is the perfect place to display a collection of colorful bowls.

741

•

Install a radiant heating system beneath a stone floor to keep feet warm in the cold winter months.

742

•

A two-tiered island gives the cook plenty of workspace and allows family or guests a seat near the action.

743

•

Add an unexpected touch of color to a professional stainless-steel range with brightly colored knobs.

744

Include open cabinetry with easy-to-open deep drawers of varying depths for pots and pans next to the stove.

745

Create a reading area in a cottage by placing a small table and a couple of chairs in front of a bookshelf.

746

Conceal television and stereo equipment behind the louvered doors of an entertainment center in a den.

747

Provide an expanse of extra storage in a home office by installing floor-to-ceiling bookshelves along one wall or around the whole room.

THE WORLD'S GREAT BALLETS
LOVE
Essential CHARLES RENNIE MACKINTOSH
DEMOCRATIC PARTY
Essential GAUDI
Richard Meier
ISRAEL 50
Oliver Messel
SOUTHERN INTERIORS
VANITY FAIR
THE FORTIES IN VOGUE
Cecil Beaton
THE SIXTIES
Gardening in a SMALL SPACE
ALMANACK
GOLF
SANTA BARBARA STYLE
ROOMS
Richard Meier Architect 2
Frank O. Gehry
BILLY BALDWIN
DIANA VREELAND

748

Craft sweet and unique pillowcases for a guest room from vintage linen.

749

Cover the windows of a bedroom with woven reed shades that can be pulled up to let in the daytime sun or closed for complete privacy at night.

750

Hang a trio of decorative antique plates on either side of a guest bed to create balance and symmetry.

751

Paint the wide-planked wood floor of a bedroom white to brighten up the room, but place a rug at the foot of the bed for warmth.

752

●

Let a chest of drawers double as a nightstand and provide extra storage space for guests.

753

●

For a clean, simple look, keep bedding to a minimum and use crisp white sheets and pillow-cases.

754

Create affordable art for a basement bedroom by framing fern fronds in a collection of flea-market frames and painting the frames in a single color.

755

•

In a guest suite, install shelving with a sliding door in front to provide a place for guests to stow away their things.

756

In a nursery, use an open, cushion-topped changing table with shelves mounted above to provide easy access to diapers, wipes, and other baby supplies.

757

Keep children's rooms neat by housing books, toys, and art supplies in fabric-lined baskets tucked into cubbies.

758

Keep a powder room as streamlined as possible with simple hardware and accessories, and even exposed plumbing.

759

When renovating a bathroom, place the light switch near the door and at a level where you would expect it to be.

760

Install a bookshelf in an oversize bath and cover the walls with a tropical leaf wallpaper.

761

Look around for keepsakes and trinkets that have a history for you to add a personal touch to a bathroom.

762

Porcelain floor tiles are durable and inexpensive.

763

Place a pair of colorful Thai silk or cotton pillows on a porch swing to promote a lazy afternoon of relaxation and appreciation of the view.

764

Keep children's sports gear out of sight and in order by hanging vintage lockers—found at a flea market or antique store—on a wall in the garage.

765

•

Toss a throw over a table on a sunporch to give a casual country air to an al fresco table setting.

766

•

Let teak patio furniture weather naturally to an appealing silvery hue that blends into the outdoor environment.

767

Place two or three Adirondack chairs at the end of a dock as a place to sit back and enjoy a summer sunrise or sunset.

768

To preserve the lawn, install a series of stepping stones along a high-traffic path through a garden.

769

Set up pairs of lounge chairs—topped with thick cushions for extra comfort—along the sides of a pool in a lushly tropical setting.

770

•

Plant angelica and wild butter-cups in an herb garden near a picket gate.

771

Create a path through a side yard with different-sized pieces of weathered flagstone in a non-linear arrangement.

772

Place a collection of bistro chairs around a table beneath an impossibly romantic canopy of fragrant wisteria.

773

A whimsical candle-lantern over an outdoor dining table can be magical for evening meals.

Chapter 12 Natural Abode

• 751 •

• 752 •

• 759 •

• 763 •

• 766 •

• 768 •

• 771 •

• 772 •

• 777 •

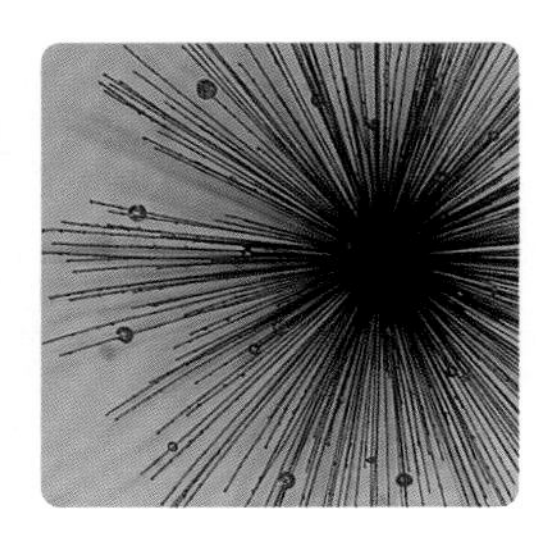
• 780 •

• 782 •

• 785 •

• 789 •

• 802 •

• 805 •

THE NATURAL ABODE is best suited for nature enthusiasts, environmentalists, and lovers of the great outdoors. This home's living, working, and eating spaces are likely to be rooms with large windows and sensational views. They're also inclined to be filled with recycled or eco-conscious materials—reclaimed wood floors, river-rock walls, organic cotton sheets. These houses invariably harmonize with their settings, fitting in with the landscape like trees in a park. And their surroundings are often naturalistic, yet laced with stone benches, fire pits, or wraparound terraces, enabling their inhabitants to commune with their surroundings and nature's splendors.

774

Install a stone, marble, or tile floor, and use nontoxic grout as a first step toward creating an environmentally friendly living room.

775

Bring the outdoors indoors by scattering a variety of plants and flowers in an open living/dining space.

776

●

Surround a modern fireplace in a renovated rustic structure with bamboo and cover the floor with slate.

777

●

Take advantage of a striking view by installing a floor-to-ceiling window wall along one side of a living room. ▶

778

●

Decorate a living room in a house in a California desert setting with furnishings and accents made of natural organic materials and a palette that complements the landscape. ▶

NATURAL WONDERS OF THE WORLD
Dia:Beacon

779

Display a pottery collection on a hand-carved pine mantel. ◂

780

Hang a chandelier made of naturally shed elk horns in front of a stone fireplace in the great room of a getaway house.

781

Create a mantel shelf with solid untreated walnut or other hardwood.

782

●

Make the most of a tropical setting by surrounding a living room with doors that open on all sides.

783

●

Top an expansive brick fireplace with an old wood beam for a rustic look. ►

784

●

Place a vase of tall, cheerful sunflowers in front of a fireplace in the warmer months. ►

BARNETT NEWMAN

785

Construct a glass enclosure to form a protected living room within the shell of an old barn that's been converted into a house.

786

Have a custom-designed table built from solid mahogany and protect it with a water-based sealant.

787

Choose upholstered dining room chairs filled with natural cotton or wool rather than synthetic polyurethane foam.

788

•

Top an outdoor dining table with natural elements, here tall wooden candle holders carved in the shape of tree branches.

789

Top dining room chairs with linen slipcovers for easy cleaning and so that you can change the look of the room with new slipcovers. ◄

790

Place a flowering plant potted in an urn in front of a mirror for double the greenery. ◄

791

Surround a dining room with floor-to-ceiling glass walls so that it appears to float in a forested setting.

792

Construct open shelves on open supports to permit views into an adjoining room and an ocean or river view beyond.

793

Use reclaimed wood to cover the floor of a charming country kitchen for a rustic look and feel.

794

Divide a large kitchen into distinct rooms with area rugs that both contrast with and complement each other.

795

Top an island with a trio of small potted citrus trees to add a tropical, cheery touch to a kitchen.

796

Lend warmth with a mix of natural materials, including both dark and light wood.

797

Create an eye-catching backsplash using brightly colored tiles in a small kitchen with little natural light. ▶

798

•

Give a modern kitchen rich, earthy appeal with stark mahogany cabinetry, narrow open shelves, and limestone floors.

799

•

Install a pivoting window over the kitchen sink to add a bounce of light from an adjoining room.

800

Call attention to a magnificent view from a den by framing glass doors with vibrant red floor-length draperies made of a natural material like wool gabardine.

801

Add a unique touch to a den by placing a dramatic lamp on a side table between a sofa and small chair.

802

Fill a cabinet with an artfully arranged collection of shells and coral, and other keepsakes.

803

A wall that bows a bit or a floor that has settled will make an old room feel graceful rather than brand new.

804

Enjoy natural beauty while you work by placing a console and X-based ottoman in front of a window overlooking an amazing view.

805

Exchange a bulky computer for a sleek laptop in a home office to avoid clutter.

806

•

Top a bed with sheets made from 100-percent organic cotton or silk and blankets of natural undyed wool.

807

•

Indulge guests by framing a spectacular landscape with a large window in a guest room.

808

Add warmth to a bedroom by topping an ornately designed wicker bed with plaid wool linens.

809

Use traditional milk paint to avoid the effects of harmful volatile organic compounds in a guest bedroom.

810

Create a tree-house atmosphere in a contemporary bedroom by covering walls with grass cloth and installing ebony-stained beadboard on a vaulted ceiling.

811

Avoid down pillows or comforters because they offer a haven for dust mites.

812

Bring the outdoors in by covering the floor of a bedroom with slate that matches an exterior patio beyond a glass window wall.

813

Hide steel support beams behind weathered wood for a more natural look in an open bedroom with sparse, modern furniture.

814

Use natural materials—such as limestone walls, 100-percent cotton towels, and linen shades—in a bathroom.

815

Add a view of the outdoors with a window over a bathtub, but mount a roman shade for privacy.

816

Put a charming antique farm table into service as a counter for a basin in a country-style bathroom.

817

Use a handwoven basket to stash fresh towels. Store it on the bathroom counter or on the floor next to the bathtub.

818

Build an upstairs outdoor deck near—and partially under—the roof of a house.

819

Accent the rustic charm of a renovated barn with a totally modern staircase leading from a stone patio.

820

Make the most of a creekside view by orienting an enclosed sunroom with generous expanses of picture windows toward the water.

821

Commune with nature on a chilly day and stay warm at the same time by installing a kiva fireplace within a covered open-air portal.

822

Provide a comfortable place from which to enjoy a view by building a deep, covered loggia and placing an array of thickly cushioned chairs on it. ◄

823

Plant wisteria to shade a dining area loggia from the setting sun and fill the air with magical scent.

824

If you serve ribs or lobster at a summer picnic or barbeque, float some violets or wildflowers in the finger bowls that will be needed.

825

•

Define the entrance to a pueblo-style house with antique Mexican pine doors and Spanish Colonial–style lanterns.

826

•

Design an entrance courtyard to ease the transition between indoors and outdoors, and to provide a private outdoor haven.

827

•

Craft a deck from ipe, an exceptionally durable Brazilian hardwood that ages gracefully and that goes perfectly with a gorgeous ocean view. ►

828

Construct an open Anglo-Japanese–inspired gazebo to provide a quiet spot for contemplation in a naturalistic garden.

829

•

If you have a stream that is prone to flooding on your property, line its banks with stones found nearby or purchased at a local nursery.

830

Design a house that blends in with the landscape and reflects the region where it is constructed.

831

Conserve natural resources and minimize impact on the landscape by converting an old barn into a modern weekend house.

832

Treat yourself to a visual feast by planting a border of flowers and grasses, such as purple *Aster novae-angliae* 'Violetta' and silvery pink *Miscanthus* 'Flamingo,' that change colors with the arrival of a new season.

833

Plant impatiens along a winding path of closely spaced stones leading to a formal main garden.

834

Create meandering paths through a wooded property to encourage long walks and appreciation of nature.

835

Add character to a garden wall in the Southwest with a pair of antique hand-wrought wooden doors at the entrance.

836

Place a rough-hewn birdbath in a shady corner of a garden as both a work of art and a place for birds to drink and play.

837

Encourage blue aquilegias and *Euphorbia amygdaloides* 'Rubra' to seed themselves in a garden pergola for a wild, overgrown look.

838

•

Landscape the grounds of an old stone house with indigenous stone, plants, and trees.

839

•

When renovating an old house, reuse as many of the original roof tiles, bricks, and beams as possible.

840

•

Introduce a sculptural touch to a desert landscape with aged terra-cotta olive jars that echo the palette of the natural surroundings.

841

Keep the colors of flowering plants on a terrace subtle so you don't compete with a stunning view.

842

Construct a fire pit on the upper level of a tiered garden and install a long, concrete bench, topping it with plenty of cushions to provide comfort during late-night gatherings.

Chapter 13 Bold Domain

• 812 •

• 813 •

• 816 •

• 822 •

• 825 •

• 833 •

• 835 •

• 837 •

• 845 •

• 851 •

• 855 •

• 858 •

• 860 •

• 867 •

• 869 •

FOR CONTEMPORARY CULTURE MAVENS, technophiles, and those who love everything cutting-edge, there's no place like the Bold Domain. Its living spaces flow into its dining spaces, and both are probably filled with gutsy modern art, vibrant color, and conversation-piece furniture. A large, flat-screen television is probably the centerpiece of the family room, where a Tommi Parzinger lamp might stand next to a Jean-Michel Frank sofa and an animal-print rug covers the floor. Private spaces have attitude too, including children's rooms, where framed vintage French posters might add color to the walls or a hot-pink canopy might cover the bed of a budding princess. Outdoor rooms and gardens are sleek and languid with chaise longues and ultramodern party lights.

843

Make a bold statement in an entrance hall by painting walls purple and enlivening them with a quartet of colorful abstract paintings.

844

Let unusual artwork or collectibles, such as a pair of 19th-century Chinese cranes, inspire a visual narrative.

845

Create a dramatic staircase with Honduran mahogany paneling and Chippendale-inspired fretwork rails.

846

Bring an exotic touch to an otherwise understated living room with zebra-patterned cowhide rugs. ▸

PALACES OF ROME
Interiorscapes
The ROYAL PALACES of SPAIN
F. HOLLAND DAY
SUFFERING THE IDEAL
THE SHELL
ASSOULINE

847

Flank a glamorous bar table in a family room with a pair of flare-arm chairs upholstered in pale pink linen.

848

Cover the floor of a family room with a white shag rug to add texture and comfort.

849

Give a vaulted family room an air of stylish glamour by suspending a pendant fixture with an oversize modern Italian lampshade from the ceiling.

KARL BLOSSFELDT
SCHIRMER/MOSEL

850

Bring a playful touch to a sitting room by displaying a collection of contemporary art. Here, bird paintings by the artist Robert Flynn hang over a white sofa. ◄

851

Let a red-cushioned coffee table inspire an array of bold accents in a comfortable and inviting family room.

852

Consolidate your electronic devices on a universal remote control, which can coordinate the television and stereo and even draw the curtains and dim the lighting.

853

Cover the walls of a living room with a zebra-stripe wallpaper but tone down the look by hanging traditional floral paintings and a pretty oval mirror.

854

Carve out an alluring seating niche in a living room with a corner banquette covered in chartreuse moleskin and pillows made from brightly colored Indian silks.

RELIGION

855

Clad a slanted ceiling in mahogany and accentuate it with a monolithic limestone fireplace that rises to the full height of a living room.

856

Install rain-sensor windows or skylights that can detect moisture and automatically close before the carpet and furniture become soaked.

857

Set off clean, geometric furniture in a neutral room with a gutsy work of art, here an abstract painting by Ed Moses.

858

•

Cover a bergère chair in a vibrant multicolored stripe to add color and personality to a formal living room.

859

Mount an abstract work of art from the 1930s or '40s on one wall of a dining room over a sideboard, here a mid-century Tommi Parzinger.

860

Surround a wood-grained Formica table with chairs upholstered in dazzling white patent leather and hang a funky chandelier over the table to complete the look.

861

•

Create striking contrasts from floor to ceiling by mixing a brown-and-white patterned rug, white wainscoting, and a glossy coral paint color for overhead. Add accessories that combine the various colors and elements between the three layers—note the two-tone chandelier, colorful centerpiece bouquets, and sepia photographs in this dining room.

862

A blue-tiled fireplace matches the seat coverings and table linens in this bright and cheerful dining area. Bold, mismatching fabrics are pulled together by their blue color palette.

863

Set a lighthearted tone in a dining room by displaying items with visual panache. Shown here is a polka-dot Hermès vase.

864

Add energy to a dining room by mixing pieces from different eras, such as the modernist Eero Saarinen table and an 18th-century chest shown here.

865

•

Install an upholstered banquette in a dining room and top with lots of fluffy pillows to create a comfortable spot for predinner cocktails.

866

•

Install a scene-control lighting system that can provide varying levels of light in different rooms—or on specific objects, such as artwork—with the flip of a switch.

867

Enrich an austere dining room with a graphic piece of modern art and a striking lighting fixture such as this 1940s Italian mercury glass chandelier.

868

Light fixtures can provide just the color accent necessary to add excitement and warmth to a room.

869

Add charm to a French-inspired kitchen by having a whimsical trompe l'oeil painted above your modern-retro, professional stove.

BOSCH

870

Install custom-designed features to combine styles and make a kitchen unique. This island features an additional slab of marble tabletop for dining, and the cooking tools hanging against the back-splash bring traditional charm to an ultra-modern space.

871

To offset a dramatic and somewhat formal color scheme in a kitchen, add small touches of contrasting colors and patterns throughout the space. Here, the black-and-white diamond backsplash and stainless-steel stove are complemented by a single orange wall, the yellow file cab-inet, and polka dot containers bearing bright-hued contents.

872

Give a kitchen a modern look that's not sterile with a mix of Douglas fir cabinetry, oak floors, and stainless-steel countertops.

873

Install a sound system with a central control and speakers in different rooms so that you can hear classical music in the kitchen and R&B in the family room.

874

Add playful, earthy touches to a modern monochromatic kitchen: Surround an island with white faux-bamboo bar stools and accessorize in small, surprising ways with colorful foods and plants.

875

Strike a bold note over a long kitchen island with Artemide's Omega pendant lamps—reissued from the 1960s—and surround it with ultramodern stainless-steel bar stools.

876

Make the most of the space in a narrow, urban kitchen by building cabinets all the way up to the ceiling. ◄

877

Hang a large collection of copper pots near a gas cooktop for convenience and to enhance the decor. ◄

878

Spice up a modern kitchen with a tall, zesty mosaic backsplash and similarly hued dishware and cooking tools, such as the bright teapot and bowls on this stovetop.

879

Paint the interior of a tall bookshelf in a color that contrasts with the walls of an office while complementing other pieces in the room.

880

Flank a plasma television mounted above a fireplace in a den with a pair of primitive masks and cover the fireplace with a bold one-of-a-kind screen.

881

Connect all your household computers on a single, preferably wireless, home network to streamline record keeping and file sharing. This way you can create a budget spreadsheet on your computer in the den and later access it from your laptop on the terrace or in bed.

882

Go bold in an office with dark wood-paneled walls by combining richly patterned fabrics that both complement and contrast with one another.

883

In a small home office, pair a round, overscale contemporary pedestal table with an Eames Management chair in a bold color and paint the ceiling with tan and white stripes.

GRACE
ANTIQUITIES

884

Upholster a striking headboard that extends beyond the width of the bed and around both side tables in trapunto with nailhead detailing.

885

Bring a touch of glamour to a guest room with gilt-trimmed furnishings and accessories.

886

Open up a bedroom painted a rich color by leaning an oversized mirror that nearly reaches the ceiling against a bare wall.

887

•

Add zest to a guest room with bright yellow linens and some modern art and furniture.

888

•

Break from tradition and place the head of a bed against the middle of a bay window. ▶

889

•

Decorate a bedroom around the style of a central piece of artwork. In this child's room, each color is pulled from the framed vintage posters on the wall, from the yellow curtains and the blue linens to the striped headboard and spotted rug. ▶

CARL LAEMMLE
LON
CHANEY
NORMAN
KERRY
MARY
PHILBIN
5000 others
"THE PHANTOM
OF THE OPERA"
DIRECTED BY
RUPERT JULIAN
A UNIVERSAL PRODUCTION
GASTON LEROUX
CREATURE
FROM THE
BLACK LAGOON
RICHARD CARLSON · JULIA ADAMS

890

●

Pair hot pink and neon green—or other favorite colors of the resident child— to make a girl's room bright and cheerful.

891

●

Give punch to a teen's room with bright color, a checker-board floor, a cozy tucked-away window seat, and a lamp made from an antique mannequin's head.

892

Create a canopy that suggests a safari tent over the bed in a boy's bedroom. Add to the theme with an animal-print rug on the floor at the end of the bed.

893

•

Drape fabric with a strong graphic pattern behind a colorful headboard and have custom bed linens made to complement both.

894

Top a chest of drawers in a master bedroom with a colorful pair of 1960s porcelain foo dogs.

895

Upholster a headboard in the same floral-print fabric as the bedskirt and tone down the look with simple linens in solid colors.

896

●

Install an undulating two-sink vanity and a supersize steel tub in a modern bathroom.

897

Install a concrete shower tub—with a built-in bench—alongside a wall of swimming pool tiles for a bold, clean look.

898

Add Hollywood glamour to a master bathroom with iridescent glass mosaic tiles in an oversize shower with multiple shower heads.

899

Add a vanity to a bathroom so that makeup doesn't have to be applied while leaning over a sink.

900

Build a pool house inspired by the style of a Japanese tea-house and decorated with plenty of outdoor furniture.

901

Craft a contemporary pool pavilion on a deck overlooking the ocean by stretching sailcloth over a steel-framed cube.

902

Surround two sides of a master bedroom suite with a covered terrace that overlooks an expansive view on one side and a pool on the other.

903

Contain an open-air porch with grommetted curtain panels that can be opened and closed with ease.

904

Position four custom chairs with thick cushions covered in brightly colored fabric around a narrow coffee table on a sun porch.

905

Set some brightly painted French iron spoon chairs at either end of a sturdy teak farm table on a covered terrace.

906

Construct a dramatic fireplace at one end of a patio, place a coffee table in front of it, and surround it with stylish teak sofas and chairs.

907

Create a splendid vista with arched hedges that lead the eye from one part of a garden to another.

908

Recreate the south of France on a rooftop terrace with a painted latticework and delicate herbs.

909

Plant highly scented plants like lavender, rosemary, and wisteria for a garden that will smell like heaven.

910

Construct a blue-bottomed infinity pool on an elevated terrace overlooking the desert hills.

911

Frame a sunken pool in an organic shape with massive, rough limestone rocks and palm trees to give the feeling of swimming on a tropical island.

JACKIE
OSCAR DE LA RENTA

Chapter 14 The Welcoming Home

• 876 • • 882 • • 885 • • 890 • • 896 •

• 903 • • 909 • • 915 • • 920 • • 925 •

• 928 • • 932 • • 940 • • 945 • • 946 •

THE WELCOMING HOME is all about comfort. Although the furniture and accessories in its living and eating areas may be new, their shapes and colors are familiar. Overstuffed sofas and chairs encourage family and friends to sit back and stay awhile. An antique or two in the living room brings out memories of an earlier generation, while a zesty paint color in a family room indulges the sensibilities of an emerging one. Guest rooms are equipped with all the comforts of home, while the master suite is the ultimate haven, with floor-length draperies, plush carpet, and upholstered reading chairs. A swing on a covered porch, picnic tables and cushioned chairs on an expansive patio, or lounge chairs in a cozy cabana offer multiple outdoor rest spots.

912

Enhance the relaxed air in a beach cottage hallway by hanging framed vintage posters with seaside themes on the wall.

913

Create an inviting window seat by topping a hidden radiator with an upholstered cushion and fluffy pillows. ◄

914

Instead of placing a coffee table in front of a sofa in a living room, use a large upholstered ottoman. ◄

915

Toss down-filled pillows onto a pair of wing chairs in a living room for added comfort.

916

Add character and warmth to a stairwell by painting walls in earthy tones and installing cream-painted wainscoting.

917

Make a large, sunny room even more inviting by upholstering a sofa and chairs in plush textured fabrics and buttery leather, adding plenty of pillows. ►

918

Create coziness in a large living room by setting up two distinct seating areas. ►

Faces of the Twentieth Century

919

Pile plenty of soft blankets in drawers beneath a window seat in a family room for easy access.

920

Carve out a cozy spot for kids in a cottage by creating a napping nook atop a platform of pull-out drawers for storing blankets.

921

Create a comfy spot to read near a window with an upholstered cushion, a bolster, a soft throw, and a side table for books and a glass of wine.

922

Establish a sense of openness by dividing rooms with partial-height walls or glass-paned doors to allow a visual connection from one room to another.

PALAZZI OF ROME
stone

MUSTIQUE
ALBERTO PINTO

923

Brighten a living room by upholstering overstuffed chairs in a windowpane check and pairing them with a custom rug inspired by a Josef Albers painting.

924

Place a few pieces of folk art or craft work from a flea market or fair on a fireplace mantel in an otherwise sparsely accented room.

925

Add color to an open, three-level foyer with an abstract wall hanging along one staircase.

926

Give energy to a traditional living room by using a fresh, youthful palette that is reflected in the walls, fabrics, and accents.

FASHION
THE CENTURY OF THE DESIGNER
THE CENTURY OF THE DESIGNER
THE ALLURE OF WOMEN
BRIGHT YOUNG THINGS
BROOKE DE OCAMPO
JONATHAN BECKER
ASSOULINE

927

•

Bring a fresh twist to an all-American palette of red, white, and blue with Asian furnishings, prints, and accents.

928

•

Cover the walls of a children's sitting room with large-scale hemp gingham and upholster a commodious chaise longue with a child-friendly acrylic fabric.

929

•

Paint the wood floor of a small living room white to make the space seem larger.

930

•

Create a casual dining space in a great room with a long picnic bench pulled up next to a simple French farm table.

931

Create warmth in a stately dining room by incorporating a mix of familiar patterns in soft colors—such as the florals, plaids, and subtle garden tones seen here.

932

Surround a dining table with high-backed upholstered chairs for long-term comfort.

933

Enrich a country table setting with a centerpiece of hydrangea, roses, and poppies in a wooden box and candle tapers placed in clear vases.

934

Mount a pair of mismatched tole trays above a fireplace for a decorative touch in a breakfast room adjoining a sunny kitchen.

935

Create a casual eating area off a kitchen by pushing an Arts and Crafts table next to a banquette and adding a couple of chairs for plenty of seating.

936

Create an inviting breakfast nook near a bay window with a lazy Susan tray, benches, and plenty of cushions covered in yellow, blue, and white fabrics.

937

Include a couple of upholstered stools, or taborets, along with a set of chairs around a dining room table to add a dash of personality.

938

•

Use a mix of seating—a cushion-topped bench, high-backed armchairs, and side chairs—around a dining table for an inviting ambience.

939

Add zing to a breakfast nook by applying black toile wall-paper above tall white pan-eling and painting the back of inset shelves lime green.

940

Keep a small kitchen bright and airy by positioning wall-mounted cabinets out of the way below ceiling level.

941

Create a country feeling in a kitchen with hardwood floors, painted cabinetry, and butter-yellow walls.

942

To vary the effects of lighting, incorporate a variety of fixture types—including pendants and under-the-cabinet lighting—and include dimmers.

943

Bring sophistication to a country-style kitchen with marble countertops, also used on a long kitchen island.

944

Paint the walls of a kitchen a bright yellow to create a cheery, welcoming atmosphere.

945

If your kitchen is short on counter space, add an oversized island in the center of the room to give you more prep room.

946

Install a comfortable window seat in a kitchen for guests and place storage baskets below.

947

If you are concerned about stains, choose easy-to-clean quartz or granite instead of marble to top an island.

948

Add a long runner in the high-traffic area of a narrow kitchen to create a soft, cozy feel.

POIS

949

Create an open kitchen that has it all—extensive food prep space, an eating area, and a place nearby for family to sit and watch television.

950

Personalize your kitchen with displays of majolica pitchers, ironstone bowls, or ceramic teapots.

951

Instead of track lighting, which draws the eye up, use an interesting table lamp with a curvy base on a desk in a home office with a low ceiling.

952

A lot of clutter can be contained behind the glass doors of a cabinet while also providing a delightful visual display.

953

•

Transform a cluttered library into an inviting haven by painting shelves and cabinets a pale sage-green, covering windows with soft shades, and adding comfortable wing chairs.

954

•

Install wall-to-wall carpet in a library for soft comfort underfoot and to cultivate a quiet environment perfect for reading.

955

•

Whip up some cushions made from vintage silk scarves to toss on a sofa for extra comfort.

956

•

Position a wing chair, ottoman, and chaise longue near a fireplace in a den for plenty of fireside seating during the chilly months.

957

Turn the top floor of a three-story house into an inviting homework/media room for teenage children.

958

Put down an equestrian-themed rug and add matching pillows on the sofa and chairs to keep a library feeling fun and family-friendly.

959

Upholster a pair of chairs in front of an enormous brick fireplace in a cozy study with a cheery striped fabric and make floor-length draperies from a sunny toile.

960

Paint the walls of a country bedroom with twin beds a pale violet-blue for a fresh and serene feeling.

961

If you like to read in bed, be sure to have an extra-big pillow to prop up and avoid a wrought-iron headboard.

962

Large benches rest at the feet of a pair of beds in a guest room, providing easy and comfortable seating.

963

•

Add comfort to a bedroom by covering the floor with a colorful and sumptuous rug.

964

•

Create a cozy spot for reading in a bedroom by placing an upholstered chair, a side table, and a reading lamp in one corner.

965

Bring charm to a guest room with sheer curtain panels, an upholstered headboard, and a ruffled bed skirt.

966

Place two beds right together—instead of separating with a table—to create a cozy guest bedroom.

967

Very pale blue walls in a guest bedroom creates a peaceful atmosphere that promotes relaxation.

968

•

Inject color and comfort in a guest room by painting the walls and headboard in vibrant hues. Include a matching pair of cozy upholstered chairs and a tea table to create an area where family and friends can sit and take in a garden view.

969

Fill a guest room with old-fashioned warmth by covering the walls with a sunny patterned fabric that matches the upholstery on a daybed.

970

•

Keep a large antique armoire made of dark wood from over-powering a bedroom by choosing one that has mirror on its doors.

971

Cover the walls and ceiling of a cozy attic bedroom in red-and-white toile and cover the bed with white linens.

972

Place a small writing desk in a window nook with a view.

JACKIE
OSCAR DE LA RENTA

973

Cover a padded headboard with striped taffeta and fashion a luxurious canopy over the head of the bed using neutral fabrics that coordinate with other objects in the room. Note the neutral colors of the shelving unit, linens, bedside table, and photo frames.

974

Place a velvet-upholstered sofa at the foot of a bed and top it with opulent pillows and a boldly patterned throw.

975

●

Fill an antique glass bottle with branches of quince to create a stunning focal point in a guest bedroom.

976

●

Cover the walls and vaulted ceiling of a guest bedroom with a cheerful floral wallpaper to create a cozy welcome.

977

For soft lighting in a bathroom, flank a mirror over the sink with sconces sporting fabric shades.

978

•

Add charm to a high-ceilinged guest bath with a floral custom-designed wallpaper.

979

•

Add a touch of spring to a powder room with potted flowering plants and miniature bouquets of fresh flowers.

980

●

Soft colors combined with just a couple garden-themed accessories (such as the little bird and plant seen here) create a warm, relaxing space in a small bathroom.

981

Set up a cozy spot in a sunroom by placing a lacquered cocktail table in front of a vintage daybed in a window corner.

982

Cover the floor of a sunroom with a boldly patterned rug that is echoed in the geometric art painted on the doors of an armoire.

983

Provide side tables and other furniture for seating nooks like this deep-cushioned iron daybed on a covered porch.

984

Install a fanciful candle chandelier on the ceiling of a covered terrace for evening enjoyment or a bit of romance.

985

Set up multiple seating areas on an expansive pea gravel patio—perfect for gatherings on warm summer nights.

986

•

Install a fireplace on an expansive porch to provide warmth on chilly evenings.

987

•

Provide cushions and blankets for porch swings—even those on a screened-in porch can get chilly.

988

Add personality to a porch with a row of rocking chairs and a band of modern pendant lamps covered in striped-fabric shades.

989

•

Drill a hole in the bottom of an old ceramic hog trough and convert it into a sink in a garden potting shed.

990

Create a multipurpose relaxation zone in a sunroom by including Anglo-Indian cane chairs, surrounding two or three sides of the room with a cushion-topped banquette, and pulling up a table and dining chairs along one portion of the banquette.

991

Install a wood stove to warm up a large sunroom even in the coldest winter months.

992

•

Position a pair of cushioned 1930s French iron chairs and side table on a terrace overlooking a formal garden and swimming pool.

993

Flank the front door of an ivy-covered stone house with agapanthus planted in pots that can be brought indoors when the weather turns cold.

994

•

Construct a wooden swing set and fort for children of all ages in the backyard.

995

•

In springtime, the fallen petals from blossoming trees will create a beautiful carpet of color on an outstretched lawn.

996

Use fine linens for a rustic picnic—the napkins won't blow away in the wind, and the juxtaposition is charming.

997

Toss a queen-size blanket or sheet on the sand to define an area for a picnic along the shore facing a summer house.

998

Press matching dish towels into service as napkins for an informal beachside brunch. ►

999

Cultivate a garden in keeping with the character of your house and any other structures on your property.

1000

Line a garden path made from different-sized stepping stones with lamb's ears and arabis.

Photo Credits

Page 2: John Gould Bessler
Page 5: Oberto Gili
Pages 6–7: Karyn R. Millet
Page 8: Karyn R. Millet
Page 9: Carlos Domenech
Page 10: Eric Piasecki
Page 11: (left) Tria Giovan
Page 11: (right) Gordon Beall
Pages 12: John Gould Bessler
Page 15: William Waldron
Page 16–17: Michel Arnaud
Page 18: Tria Giovan
Page 19: Carlos Emilio
Page 20: Tria Giovan
Page 21: Ellen McDermott
Page 22: Grey Crawford
Page 23: Laura Moss
Page 24: Roger Davies
Page 25: Pieter Estersohn
Page 26: Tim Street-Porter
Page 27: Edmund Barr
Page 28: Pieter Estersohn
Page 29: Erik Kvalsvik
Page 30: Gordon Beall
Page 31: Gordon Beall
Page 32: Fritz von der Schulenburg
Page 33: Eric Piasecki
Page 34: Tria Giovan
Page 35: Simon Upton
Page 36 (left): Simon Upton
Page 36 (right): Tim Street-Porter
Page 37: Grey Crawford
Page 38: John Gould Bessler
Page 39: Antoine Bootz
Page 40: Eric Piasecki
Page 41: Tria Giovan
Page 42: Laura Moss
Page 43: Frances Janisch
Page 44: Tim Street-Porter
Page 45: Tim Street-Porter
Page 46: Frances Janisch
Page 47: Eric Piasecki
Page 48: (left): Eric Piasecki
Page 48: (right): Dominique Vorillon
Page 49: Jeff McNamara
Page 50: Gordon Beall
Page 51: John Gould Bessler
Page 52: Ellen McDermott
Page 53: Kerri McCaffety
Page 54: Susan Gilmore
Page 55: Eric Piasecki
Page 56: Frances Janisch
Page 57: Jeremy Samuelson
Page 58: Oberto Gili
Page 59: Tim Street-Porter
Page 60: Dominique Vorillon
Page 61: Dominique Vorillon
Page 62: Eric Piasecki
Page 63: John Gould Bessler
Page 64: John Gould Bessler
Page 65: Pieter Estersohn
Page 66: Simon Upton
Page 67: Chuck Baker
Page 68: Nina Bramhall
Page 69: Vivian Russell
Page 70: John M. Hall
Page 71: Nina Bramhall
Page 72: Laura Resen
Page 75: Jack Thompson
Page 76: John Gould Bessler
Page 77: Grey Crawford
Page 78–79: Ken Hayden
Page 80: Roger Davies
Page 81: John M. Hall
Page 82: Simon Upton
Page 83: John Gould Bessler
Page 84: Tria Giovan
Page 85: Ellen McDermott
Page 86: Peter Murdock
Page 87: Peter Murdock
Page 88: Tria Giovan
Page 89: Roger Davies
Page 90: Pieter Estersohn
Page 91: Antoine Bootz
Page 92: Edmund Barr
Page 93: Hugh Stewart
Page 94: Jonn Coolidge
Page 95: Peter Murdock
Page 96: Laura Resen
Page 97: Eric Piasecki
Page 98: Pieter Estersohn
Page 99: Christopher Baker
Page 100: Simon Upton
Page 101: Antione Bootz
Page 102: Vicente Wolf
Page 103: Pieter Estersohn
Page 104: Tria Giovan
Page 105: Jonn Coolidge
Page 106: Jonn Coolidge
Page 107: Antoine Bootz
Page 108: Peter Murdock
Page 109: Laura Moss
Page 110: Tim Street-Porter
Page 111: Tria Giovan
Page 112: Jonn Coolidge
Page 113: Eric Piasecki
Page 114: John Gould Bessler
Page 115: Pieter Estersohn
Page 116: Lisa Romerein
Page 117: Eric Piasecki
Page 118: Gordon Beall
Page 119: Karyn R. Millet
Page 120: Antoine Bootz
Page 121: Tria Giovan
Page 122: Ellen McDermott
Page 123: Eric Piasecki
Page 124: Roger Davies
Page 125: Karyn R. Millet
Page 126: Tria Giovan
Page 127: Grey Crawford
Page 128: Tim Street-Porter
Page 129: John Gould Bessler
Page 130: John M. Hall
Page 131: Eric Piasecki
Page 132: Tria Giovan
Page 133: Ken Hayden
Page 134: Pieter Estersohn
Page 135: Pieter Estersohn
Page 136: Nina Bramhall
Page 137 (both): John M. Hall
Pages 138: Lisa Romerein
Page 141: Jeff McNamara

Page 142: Eric Piasecki
Page 143: Eric Piasecki
Page 144–145: Darrin Haddad
Page 146: Tim Street-Porter
Page 147: Eric Piasecki
Page 148: Karyn R. Millet
Page 149: Chuck Baker
Page 150: Eric Piasecki
Page 151: Dominique Vorillon
Page 152: Grey Crawford
Page 153: Tria Giovan
Page 154: Ellen McDermott
Page 155: Frances Janisch
Page 156: Christopher Baker
Page 157: Christopher Baker
Page 158: Carlos Emilio
Page 159: Oberto Gili
Page 160: Ken Hayden
Page 161: Don Freeman
Page 162: Jack Thompson
Page 163: John Gould Bessler
Page 164 (left): Roger Davies
Page 164 (right): Don Freeman
Page 165: Pieter Estersohn
Page 166: John Gould Bessler
Page 167: Tria Giovan
Page 168: Christopher Baker
Page 169: Eric Piasecki
Page 170: Jeff McNamara
Page 171: Ellen McDermott
Page 172: Pieter Estersohn
Page 173: Karyn R. Millet

Page 174: Eric Piasecki
Page 175: John Gould Bessler
Page 176: Jonn Coolidge
Page 177: Eric Roth
Page 178: Oberto Gili
Page 179: John Ellis
Page 180: Eric Piasecki
Page 181: Oberto Gili
Page 182: Roger Davies
Page 183: Carlos Emilio
Page 184: Oberto Gili
Page 185: Jeff McNamara
Page 186: Eric Piasecki
Page 187: Oberto Gili
Page 188: Lisa Romerein
Page 189: Don Freeman
Page 190: Tim Street-Porter
Page 191: Grey Crawford
Page 192: Christopher Baker
Page 193: Dominique Vorillon
Page 194: Roger Davies
Page 195: Eric Piasecki
Page 196: Gordon Beall
Page 197: Tim Street-Porter
Page 198: Tria Giovan
Page 199: John Ellis
Page 200: Ellen McDermott
Page 201: Eric Piasecki
Page 202: Tim Street-Porter
Page 203: Dominique Vorillon
Page 204: John M. Hall
Page 205: Christopher Baker

Page 206: Lisa Romerein
Page 207: Laura Moss
Page 208: Don Freeman
Page 209: Tria Giovan
Page 210: John Gould Bessler
Page 211: Lisa Romerein
Page 212: Peter Murdock
Page 213: Simon Upton
Pages 214–215: Roger Foley
Page 216: Christopher Baker
Page 217: John M. Hall
Pages 218: John Gould Bessler
Page 221: Don Freeman
Page 222–223: William Waldron
Page 224: Christopher Baker
Page 225: Ellen McDermott
Page 226: Lambrose Photography
Page 227: Lambrose Photography
Page 228: Ellen McDermott
Page 229: Eric Piasecki
Page 230: John Gould Bessler
Page 231: Erik Kvalsvik
Page 232: Roger Davies
Page 233: Ellen McDermott
Page 234: Roger Davies
Page 235 (left): Karyn R. Millet
Page 235 (right): Ellen McDermott
Page 236: Tria Giovan
Page 237: Jeff McNamara

Page 238: Eric Piasecki
Page 239: Roger Davies
Page 240: Andreas von Einsiedel
Page 241: Roger Davies
Page 242: John Gould Bessler
Page 243: Jack Thompson
Page 244: Tria Giovan
Page 245: Karyn R. Millet
Page 246: John Gould Bessler
Page 247: Don Freeman
Page 248: Oberto Gili
Page 249: Tara Striano
Page 250: Tim Street-Porter
Page 251: Eric Piasecki
Page 252: Don Freeman
Page 253: Roger Davies
Page 254: Ken Hayden
Page 255: Oberto Gili
Page 256: Christopher Baker
Page 257: Paul Whicheloe
Page 258: Tim Street-Porter
Page 259: Christopher Baker
Page 260: Simon Upton
Page 261: Don Freeman
Page 262: John Gould Bessler
Page 263: John Gould Bessler
Page 264: Peter Murdock
Page 265: John Gould Bessler
Page 266: Gordon Beall
Page 267: John Gould Bessler
Page 268: Lisa Romerein
Page 269: Jeff McNamara

Page 270: John Gould Bessler
Page 271: Oberto Gili
Page 272: Hugh Stewart
Page 273: Oberto Gili
Page 274: Susan Gilmore
Page 275: Lisa Romerein
Page 276: Tria Giovan
Page 277: Oberto Gili
Page 278: Karyn R. Millet
Page 279: Lisa Romerein
Page 280: Gridley + Graves
Page 281: Gridley + Graves
Page 282: Simon Upton
Page 283: Roger Davies
Page 284: Laura Resen
Page 285: John Gould Bessler
Page 286: Victoria Pearson
Page 287: Christopher Baker
Page 288: Roger Davies
Page 289: Karyn R. Millet
Page 290: Christopher Baker
Page 291: Victoria Pearson
Page 292: Frances Janisch
Page 293: Christopher Baker
Page 294: Tim Street-Porter
Page 295: Tria Giovan
Page 296: Marion Brenner
Page 297 (left): Vivian Russell
Page 297 (right): Curtice Taylor
Pages 298: Tria Giovan
Page 301: Tria Giovan
Page 302: Christopher Baker

Page 303: Susan Gilmore
Page 304: Simon Upton
Page 305: Simon Upton
Page 306: Roger Davies
Page 307: Frances Janisch
Page 308: Laura Moss
Page 309: Jonn Coolidge
Page 310: Susan Gilmore
Page 311: Tria Giovan
Page 312: Tim Street-Porter
Page 313: Eric Piasecki
Page 314: Tria Giovan
Page 315: Karyn R. Millet
Page 316: Tria Giovan
Page 317: John Gould Bessler
Page 318: John Gould Bessler
Page 319: Grey Crawford
Pages 320–321: Karyn R. Millet
Page 322: Karyn R. Millet
Page 323: Miki Duisterhof
Page 324: Roger Davies
Page 325: Frances Janisch
Page 326: Frances Janisch
Page 327: Michel Arnaud
Page 328: Eric Piasecki
Page 329: Laura Moss
Page 330: Eric Piasecki
Page 331: Karyn R. Millet
Page 332: Tria Giovan
Page 333: Grey Crawford
Page 334: Tim Street-Porter
Page 335: Kerri McCaffety
Page 336: Eric Piasecki
Page 337: Frances Janisch
Page 338: Eric Piasecki
Page 339: Roger Davies
Page 340: J. Savage Gibson
Page 341: Eric Piasecki
Page 342: Jeff McNamara
Page 343: Tria Giovan
Page 344: Antoine Bootz
Page 345: Tim Street-Porter
Page 346: Eric Piasecki
Page 347: Frances Janisch
Page 348: Dominique Vorillon
Page 349: Laura Moss
Page 350: Ann Stratton
Page 351: John Gould Bessler
Page 352: Susan Gilmore
Page 353: Eric Piasecki
Page 354: Nina Bramhall
Page 355: John M. Hall
Pages 356: Victoria Pearson
Page 359: Michel Arnaud
Page 360: Simon Upton
Page 361: Paul Whicheloe
Page 362–363: Paul Whicheloe
Page 364: Simon Upton
Page 365: Ellen McDermott
Page 366: Tria Giovan
Page 367: Frances Janisch
Page 368: Eric Roth
Page 369: John Ellis
Page 370: J. Savage Gibson
Page 371: Oberto Gili
Page 372: John Gould Bessler
Page 373: Gordon Beall
Page 374: Karyn R. Millet
Page 375: Pieter Estersohn
Page 376: John Ellis
Page 377: Victoria Pearson
Page 378: Eric Piasecki
Page 379: Simon Upton
Page 380: Peter Murdock
Page 381: William Waldron
Page 382: John Gould Bessler
Page 383: Roger Davies
Page 384: Jeff McNamara
Page 385: Frances Janisch
Pages 386–387: Roger Davies
Page 388: John Gould Bessler
Page 389: Eric Piasecki
Page 390: J. Savage Gibson
Page 391: Andreas von Einsiedel
Page 392: Pieter Estersohn
Page 393: Ken Hayden
Page 394: Carlos Emilio
Page 395: Antoine Bootz
Page 396: Tria Giovan
Page 397: Frances Janisch
Page 398: Ray Kachatorian
Page 399: Eric Piasecki
Page 400: Pieter Estersohn
Page 401: Pieter Estersohn
Page 402: Christopher Baker
Page 403: Karyn R. Millet
Page 404: Don Freeman
Page 405: Frances Janisch
Page 406: John Gould Bessler
Page 407: Erik Kvalsvik
Page 408: Victoria Pearson
Page 409: Tria Giovan
Page 410: Tim Street-Porter
Page 411: Simon Upton
Page 412: Eric Piasecki
Page 413: Eric Piasecki
Page 414: Eric Piasecki
Page 415: Peter Murdock
Page 416: Peter Murdock
Page 417: John Gould Bessler
Page 418: Dominique Vorillon
Page 419: Charles Maraia
Page 420 (left): Dominique Vorillon
Page 420 (right): San An
Page 421: Eric Piasecki
Page 422: John Gould Bessler
Page 423: Christopher Baker
Page 424: Brendan Paul
Page 425: Grey Crawford
Page 426: Pieter Estersohn
Page 427: Tim Beddow
Page 428: Ken Hayden
Page 429: Nick Sargent
Page 430: John M. Hall
Page 431: Marion Brenner
Pages 432: Karyn R. Millet
Page 435: Grey Crawford
Page 436: Roger Davies
Page 437: Eric Piasecki
Page 438: Eric Piasecki
Page 439: Edmund Barr
Page 440: Jeff McNamara
Page 441: Eric Piasecki
Page 442: Don Freeman
Page 443: Roger Davies
Page 444: Tria Giovan
Page 445: Tria Giovan
Page 446: Andreas von Einsiedel
Page 447: Dominique Vorillon
Page 448: Frances Janisch
Page 449: Paul Whicheloe
Page 450: Carlos Emilio
Page 451: Lisa Romerein
Page 452: John Ellis
Page 453: Gordon Beall
Page 454: Don Freeman
Page 455: Ken Hayden
Page 456: Roger Davies
Page 457: Brendan Paul
Page 458: Dominique Vorillon
Page 459: Charles Maraia
Page 460: Roger Davies
Page 461: J. Savage Gibson
Page 462: John Gould Bessler
Page 463: Brendan Paul
Page 464: Christopher Baker
Page 465: Dominique Vorillon
Page 466: Tria Giovan
Page 467: John M. Hall

Page 468 (left): Tria Giovan
Page 468 (right): Eric Piasecki
Page 469: Laura Resen
Page 470: Ken Hayden
Page 471: Charles Maraia
Page 472: Karyn R. Millet
Page 473: Jonathan Wallen
Page 474: Grey Crawford
Page 475: John Gould Bessler
Page 476: Gridley + Graves
Page 477: Tria Giovan
Page 478: Tria Giovan
Page 479: Eric Piasecki
Page 480: Karyn R. Millet
Page 481: Ray Kachatorian
Page 482: Jonathan Wallen
Page 483: Tim Street-Porter
Page 484: Karyn R. Millet
Page 485: Tim Street-Porter
Page 486: Ray Kachatorian
Page 487: J. Savage Gibson
Page 488: Kerri McCaffety
Page 489: Laura Moss
Page 490: Eric Piasecki
Page 493: Gordon Beall
Page 494: Eric Piasecki
Page 495: Gordon Beall
Page 496: Gordon Beall
Page 497: Don Freeman
Page 498: Gordon Beall
Page 499: Gordon Beall
Page 500: Antoine Bootz
Page 501: Antoine Bootz
Page 502: Tria Giovan
Page 503: Thibault Jeanson
Page 504: Eric Piasecki
Page 505: John Gould Bessler
Page 506: Antoine Bootz
Page 507: Don Freeman
Page 508: Oberto Gili
Page 509: Roger Davies
Page 510: Thibault Jeanson
Page 511: Don Freeman
Page 512: Eric Piasecki
Page 513: Tim Clinch
Page 514: Hugh Stewart
Page 515: Tria Giovan
Page 516: Tim Street-Porter
Page 517: Ann Stratton
Page 518: Don Freeman
Page 519: Hugh Stewart
Page 520: Jeremy Samuelson
Page 521: John Ellis
Page 522: Don Freeman
Page 523: Roger Davies
Page 524: Thibault Jeanson
Page 525: Jeremy Samuelson
Page 526: Brendan Paul and Darrin Haddad
Page 527: Roger Davies
Page 528: Don Freeman
Page 529: Gordon Beall
Page 530: Jacques Dirand
Page 531: John M. Hall
Page 532: Eric Piasecki
Page 533: Tim Clinch
Page 534: Tim Clinch
Page 535: Don Freeman
Page 536: Tim Street-Porter
Page 537: Don Freeman
Page 538: Thibault Jeanson
Page 539: Eric Piasecki
Page 540: Tim Clinch
Page 541: Eric Piasecki
Page 542: Thibault Jeanson
Page 543: Thibault Jeanson
Page 544: Simon Upton
Page 545: Don Freeman
Page 547: Fernando Bengoechea
Page 548: Don Freeman
Page 549: John Ellis
Page 550: Tim Street-Porter
Page 551: Don Freeman
Page 552: Jeremy Samuelson
Page 553: Frances Janisch
Page 554: Thibault Jeanson
Page 555: Tim Street-Porter
Page 556: Leah Fasten
Page 557: Don Freeman
Page 558: Oberto Gili
Page 559: Tim Clinch
Page 560: Ann Stratton
Page 561: Tria Giovan
Page 562: John M. Hall
Page 563: Mick Hales
Page 564: John M. Hall
Page 565: Nina Bramhall
Page 566: Gordon Beall
Page 567: John M. Hall
Page 568: Tim Street-Porter
Page 569: Vivian Russell
Page 570: John M. Hall
Page 572: Vicente Wolf
Page 575: Eric Piasecki
Page 576: Gordon Beall
Page 577: Tim Beddow
Page 578: Eric Piasecki
Page 579: Eric Piasecki
Page 580: Simon Upton
Page 581: Tim Street-Porter
Page 582: Grey Crawford
Page 583: Roger Davies
Page 584: Eric Piasecki
Page 585: Oberto Gili
Page 586: Eric Piasecki
Page 587: Ray Kachatorian
Page 588: Roger Davies
Page 589: Roger Davies
Page 590: Simon Upton
Page 591: Ray Kachatorian
Page 592: Tim Beddow
Page 593: J. Savage Gibson
Page 594: Oberto Gili
Page 595: Eric Piasecki
Page 596: Eric Piasecki
Page 597: Jonn Coolidge
Page 598: Tim Beddow
Page 599: Tria Giovan
Page 600: Lizzie Himmel
Page 601: John Gould Bessler
Page 602: Eric Piasecki
Page 603: Gordon Beall
Page 604: Gordon Beall
Page 605: Eric Roth
Page 606: Oberto Gili
Page 607: Kerri McCaffety
Page 608: Simon Upton
Page 610: Tim Beddow
Page 611: Eric Piasecki
Page 612: Gordon Beall
Page 614: Tria Giovan
Page 615: Oberto Gili
Page 616: Ray Kachatorian
Page 617: Vicente Wolf
Page 618: Simon Upton
Page 620: Tim Beddow
Page 621: John Gould Bessler
Page 622: Laura Resen
Page 623: Thibault Jeanson
Page 624: Melanie Acevedo
Page 625: Tim Beddow
Page 626: Grey Crawford
Page 627: Gordon Beall
Page 628: Eric Piasecki
Page 629: Kerri McCaffety
Page 630: Mick Hales
Page 631: Eric Crichton/Corbis
Page 632: Gordon Beall
Page 635: Timothy Bell
Page 636: Grey Crawford

Page 638: Jonn Coolidge
Page 639: Vicente Wolf
Page 640: Jack Thompson
Page 641: Eric Boman
Page 642: Roger Davies
Page 643: Carlos Domenech
Page 644: Jack Thompson
Page 645: Gordon Beall
Page 646: Steve Freihon
Page 647: Tria Giovan
Page 648: Jack Thompson
Page 649: Tria Giovan
Page 650: Roger Davies
Page 651: Christopher Baker
Page 652: Jonn Coolidge
Page 653: Vicente Wolf
Page 654: Christopher Baker
Page 655: Carlos Domenech
Page 656: Tria Giovan
Page 657: Jack Thompson
Page 658: John Gould Bessler
Page 659: Peter Murdock
Page 660: John Gould Bessler
Page 661: Roger Davies
Page 662: John M. Hall
Page 663: Eric Piasecki
Page 664: Jack Thompson
Page 665: Gordon Beall
Page 666: Grey Crawford
Page 667: Jonn Coolidge
Page 668: Gordon Beall
Page 669: Jack Thompson
Page 670: Gordon Beall
Page 671: Tria Giovan
Page 672: Karyn R. Millet
Page 674: Vicente Wolf
Page 675: Jack Thompson
Page 676: Karyn R. Millet
Page 677: Roger Davies
Page 678: Eric Piasecki
Page 679: Gordon Beall
Page 680: Oberto Gili
Page 681: Grey Crawford
Page 682: John Gould Bessler
Page 684: Oberto Gili
Page 685: Jack Thompson
Page 686: Roger Davies
Page 687: Jack Thompson
Page 688: Jack Thompson
Page 689: Mick Hales
Page 690: Tim Beddow
Page 691: Mick Hales
Page 692: Gordon Beall
Page 695: William Waldron
Page 696: Christopher Baker
Page 697: Brendan Paul
Page 699: Hugh Stewart
Page 700: Timothy Bell
Page 701: Steve Freihon
Page 702: Erik Kvalsvik
Page 704: Paul Whicheloe
Page 705: Paul Whicheloe
Page 706: Grey Crawford
Page 707: Don Freeman
Page 708: Antoine Bootz
Page 710: Grey Crawford
Page 711: Laura Moss
Page 712: Karyn R. Millet
Page 714: Christopher Baker
Page 715: Erik Kvalsvik
Page 716: Lambros Photography Inc.
Page 717: Kerri McCaffety
Page 718: Ellen McDermott
Page 719: J. Savage Gibson
Page 720: Peter Murdock
Page 722: Peter Murdock
Page 723: Joshua McHugh
Page 724: J. Savage Gibson
Page 725: Ben Duggan
Page 726: Brendan Paul
Page 727: J. Savage Gibson
Page 728: Don Freeman
Page 729: Steve Freihon
Page 730: Brendan Paul
Page 731: Gordon Beall
Page 732: Fred Lyon
Page 733: Fred Lyon
Page 734: Gordon Beall
Page 735: Jeff McNamara
Page 736: Ray Kachatorian
Page 737: Gordon Beall
Page 738: Hugh Stewart
Page 739: Christopher Baker
Page 740: Christopher Baker
Page 742: Roger Davies
Page 743: Grey Crawford
Page 744: Vivian Russell
Page 746: Gordon Beall
Page 747: Ray Kachatorian
Page 748: Erik Kvalsvik
Page 751: Edmund Barr
Page 752: Karyn R. Millet
Page 754: Erik Kvalsvik
Page 755: Dominique Vorillon
Page 756: Tria Giovan
Page 757: Oberto Gili
Page 758: Jonn Coolidge
Page 759: Tim Beddow
Page 760: Erik Kvalsvik
Page 762: Edmund Barr
Page 763: Oberto Gili
Page 764: Karyn R. Millet
Page 765: Erik Kvalsvik
Page 766: Erik Kvalsvik
Page 767: J. Savage Gibson
Page 768: Eric Piasecki
Page 769: John Ellis
Page 770: Laura Moss
Page 771: Grey Crawford
Page 772: Roger Davies
Page 773: Ben Duggan
Page 774: Edmund Barr
Page 775: Oberto Gili
Page 776: J. Savage Gibson
Page 777: Grey Crawford
Page 778: Erik Kvalsvik
Page 780: Grey Crawford
Page 781: Tria Giovan
Page 782: Erik Kvalsvik
Page 783: Erik Kvalsvik
Page 784: Christopher Baker
Page 785: Tria Giovan
Page 786: Tria Giovan
Page 787: Tim Beddow
Page 788: Tria Giovan
Page 789: Oberto Gili
Page 790: Vincent Motte
Page 791: Nina Bramhall
Page 792: Tria Giovan
Page 793: Erik Kvalsvik
Page 794: Curtice Taylor
Page 795: John M. Hall
Page 796: Mick Hales
Page 797: Tim Street-Porter
Page 798: Nina Bramhall
Page 799: Vivian Russell
Page 800: Roger Davies
Page 801: Tim Beddow
Page 802: Karyn R. Millet
Page 803: Mick Hales
Page 804: Tim Street-Porter
Page 806: Eric Roth
Page 809: Gordon Beall
Page 810: Grey Crawford
Page 811: Grey Crawford
Page 812: Gordon Beall
Page 813: Gordon Beall
Page 814: Tria Giovan
Page 815: Jeremy Samuelson

Page 816: Eric Piasecki
Page 817: Eric Roth
Page 818: Dominique Vorillon
Page 820: Jonn Coolidge
Page 822: Tria Giovan
Page 823: Jonn Coolidge
Page 824: Jonn Coolidge
Page 825: Gordon Beall
Page 826: Jeff McNamara
Page 827: Jeff McNamara
Page 828: Tria Giovan
Page 829: Tria Giovan
Page 830: Gordon Beall
Page 831: Jonn Coolidge
Page 832: Grey Crawford
Page 833: Lizzie Himmel
Page 834: Jonn Coolidge
Page 836: John Ellis
Page 837: Grey Crawford
Page 838: John M. Hall
Page 840: Martyn Gallina-Jones
Page 841: John Ellis
Page 842: Bob Heimstra
Page 843: Gordon Beall
Page 844: Michael James O'Brien
Page 845: Ben Duggan
Page 846: Eric Roth
Page 847: Gordon Beall
Page 848: Gordon Beall
Page 849: Grey Crawford
Page 850: Eric Piasecki
Page 851: Gordon Beall
Page 852: Eric Roth
Page 853: Antoine Bootz
Page 854: Grey Crawford
Page 855: Tria Giovan
Page 856: Antoine Bootz
Page 857: Pieter Estersohn
Page 858: Gordon Beall
Page 859: Mick Hales
Page 860: Oberto Gili
Page 861: Oberto Gili
Page 862: Eric Roth
Page 864: Tim Street-Porter
Page 865: Tim Street-Porter
Page 866: John M. Hall
Page 867: Pieter Estersohn
Page 868: Dominique Vorillon
Page 869: Eric Piasecki
Page 870: Dominique Vorillon
Page 873: Victoria Pearson
Page 874: Tria Giovan
Page 875: Victoria Pearson
Page 876: Hugh Stewart
Page 877: J. Savage Gibson
Page 878: Ann Stratton
Page 879: Victoria Pearson
Page 880: J. Savage Gibson
Page 881: Tria Giovan
Page 882: Antoine Bootz
Page 883: J. Savage Gibson
Page 884: Antoine Bootz
Page 885: Dominique Vorillon
Page 886: Dominique Vorillon
Page 888: Roger Davies
Page 889: J. Savage Gibson
Page 890: Tria Giovan
Page 891: Oberto Gili
Page 892: Don Freeman
Page 894: J. Savage Gibson
Page 895: Gordon Beall
Page 896: Eric Piasecki
Page 897: Roger Davies
Page 898: Erik Kvalsvik
Page 899: Dominique Vorillon
Page 900: Laura Moss
Page 901: Ellen McDermott
Page 902: Dominique Vorillon
Page 903: Gordon Beall
Page 904: Oberto Gili
Page 906: Paul Whicheloe
Page 907: Buff Strickland
Page 908: Brendan Paul
Page 909: Erik Kvalsvik
Page 910: Grey Crawford
Page 911: Tria Giovan
Page 912: Tim Beddow
Page 914: Don Freeman
Page 915: Brendan Paul
Page 916: Victoria Pearson
Page 918: Gordon Beall
Page 919: Jonn Coolidge
Page 920: Tim Clinch
Page 921: Gordon Beall
Page 922: J. Savage Gibson
Page 923: Oberto Gili
Page 924: Dominique Vorillon
Page 925: Erik Kvalsvik
Page 926: Don Freeman
Page 927: Gordon Beall
Page 928: Pieter Estersohn
Page 929: Brendan Paul
Page 930: Gordon Beall
Page 931: Antoine Bootz
Page 932: Ray Kachatorian
Page 933: Gordon Beall
Page 934: Tim Street-Porter
Page 935: J. Savage Gibson
Page 936: Gordon Beall
Page 937: J. Savage Gibson
Page 938: Christopher Baker
Page 940: Ray Kachatorian
Page 941: Nina Bramhall
Page 942: Roger Davies
Page 943: John M. Hall
Page 944: Laura Moss
Page 945: Laura Moss
Page 946: Nina Bramhall
Page 947: Nina Bramhall

Index

A
Abstraction, 410, 413, 414
Accents, 20, 25, 30, 77, 78–79, 361, 513, 582, 626
Airiness, 98
Albers, Josef, 883
Alcoves, 676
Antiques stores, 277
Appliances, 229, 233, 420
Arbors, 296, 431
Arcades, 216
Architectural ornaments, 128, 194,196, 340
Armoires, 444, 552, 587, 623, 922, 931
Art Deco, 210
Artwork, 50, 52–53, 58–59, 164, 168, 195, 197, 200, 203–204, 209, 273, 285, 325, 342, 345, 371, 373, 410, 415, 466–467, 472–473, 541, 578, 607, 646, 821, 823, 825, 831, 848

B
Backsplashes, 232, 267, 309, 310, 349, 376, 598, 711, 715, 768, 834, 841
Balance, 12–71
Banquettes, 241, 242, 262, 330, 596, 654, 817, 830, 878, 895, 939
Barn stars, 368, 475
Barns, 213, 761, 783, 792
Baskets, 254, 449, 583, 733, 781, 903
Bathrooms, 26, 64–65, 90–91, 104, 119, 131, 164–165, 210–211, 352, 383, 442, 462–463, 478, 556–558, 621–624, 681–684, 734–735, 780–781, 856–858, 927–929
Bathtubs, 556, 558, 684, 856, 857
Beadboard, 624, 713, 777
Beads, 346
Beams, 24, 27, 202, 304, 353, 370
Bed canopies, 187, 189, 336, 399, 457–459
Bed curtains, 271, 335–336
Bed linens, 549, 553, 679, 726, 729, 774, 776, 777, 848, 853, 854, 878, 923, 925, 944
Bedrooms, 47–49, 89, 117–118, 158–162, 175, 187–193, 208–209, 255–257, 314–315, 332–338, 378–382, 392, 399, 402–405, 407, 422, 440–441, 450–454, 457–461, 541–555, 610–620, 668–680, 726–733, 774–779, 846–855
  children's, 46, 191, 209, 251, 400–401, 406, 477, 552, 553, 668, 732, 733, 851, 852, 914–926
  guest, 39, 48, 187, 208, 252, 333, 351, 381, 453–454, 848, 851
Beds, 46, 48, 49, 117–118, 176, 190–193, 252, 256, 399, 401, 453–454, 456–460, 481, 610, 613, 619, 776, 848, 918, 919, 921
  canopied, 545, 547, 548, 554, 555,615, 852, 915, 925
  curtained, 551, 679, 680
  day, 930, 932
  upholstered, 493, 596, 655, 925
Bedspreads, 618
Belin, Valerie, 578
Benches, 99, 235, 245, 354, 400, 405, 451, 454, 554, 588, 616, 620, 805, 889, 897, 898
Bins, 600
Birdbaths, 798
Bold domains, 806–869
  bathrooms, 856–858
  bedrooms, 846–855
  characteristics of, 808
  dining rooms and breakfast nooks, 823–832
  gardens, 866–869
  kitchens and pantries, 833–841
  libraries, dens, and offices, 842–845
  living spaces, 809–822
  outdoor rooms and sun rooms, 859–865
Bookshelves, 609, 665, 701, 723, 724, 733, 735, 842, 907
Bottles, 601, 926
Bowls, 719, 905
Boxes, 254, 449, 645
Braid, 326, 327
Brass, 416
Breakfast nooks, 37, 45, 60, 102, 153,245, 278, 330, 419, 518, 521, 596, 707, 710, 894, 895, 897, 899, 905
Brick, 488
Brooks, 631, 791
Bureaus, 253, 405
Burlap, 147
Busts, 534, 667

C
Cabinets, 257, 290, 342, 400, 772, 906, 907
  hardware for, 531, 734
  kitchen, 83–85, 155, 228–229, 375, 437, 531, 599, 602, 660, 663, 664, 711, 719, 722, 770, 836, 841, 900
  medicine, 622
Candles and candleholders, 288, 560, 645, 747, 763, 893, 932
Candlesticks, 59
Carpets, 49, 77, 105, 108, 110, 112, 133,179, 182–184, 221, 224, 260, 328, 360, 394–395, 397, 407–408, 414, 461, 505, 539, 545, 588, 642, 703, 714, 728, 767, 812, 852, 883, 903, 911, 931
  Chinese, 535
  hand-hooked, 509
  Oriental, 558, 603, 606, 649
  Persian, 508, 584, 620
  Samarkand, 917

wall-to-wall, 907
zebra-patterned, 541, 582, 810
Cedar, 486
Ceilings, 142, 160, 258, 365, 373, 423, 435, 442–443, 510, 540, 551, 579, 686, 706, 713, 777, 819, 844, 923, 926
Centerpieces, 350, 595
Chairs, 34, 36–37, 44, 45, 52, 97–98, 100–102, 150, 167, 238, 240, 242–244, 320, 331, 371, 384–385, 390–391, 410, 447, 521, 528, 587, 595, 598, 652, 668, 676, 686, 706, 786, 812, 824, 863, 864, 876, 883, 898, 917, 920, 940
Adirondack, 741
American West, 610
bamboo, 588
Bergère, 822
bistro, 747
cane, 939
Chippendale, 521
coverings, 262, 265, 331, 396–398, 436, 447–448
dining room, 518, 521, 523, 591, 654, 656, 762, 765, 891, 898, 939
director's, 709
Eames Management, 844
Edwardian, 665
folding, 707
legs, 316
Louis XV, 584
Regency, 518, 537
rocking, 936
spoon, 864
wicker, 688
wingback, 535, 556, 576, 649,667, 875, 907, 908
Chaise longues, 39, 166, 541, 625, 626, 671, 742, 888, 908
Chandeliers, 33, 37, 45, 54, 76, 78–79, 153, 184, 194, 202, 205–207, 278–279, 329, 346, 368, 372, 436, 511, 551, 576, 582, 587, 591, 600, 652, 658, 706, 757, 824, 831, 932
Changing tables, 732
Checks, 336, 379, 381
Cheerfulness, 412, 423
Chests, 584, 829
decoupaged, 616
hand-painted, 555, 611
China. *See* Dishes.
China cabinets, 21, 227, 281, 348, 418, 437, 450
Chinoiserie, 206, 279, 344, 396–397
Closets, 257
Clothing, Chinese, 332
Cocktails, 420
Colors and color schemes, 15, 19, 22, 30–31, 36, 40, 49, 52, 55, 64, 75, 77, 78–79, 80, 82, 85, 89, 96, 122, 133, 143, 146, 174, 183, 195, 224, 229, 236, 238, 252, 258, 261, 276, 283, 287, 302–303, 311, 319, 322–323, 336, 356–431, 435, 437, 480, 538, 540, 566, 622, 661, 668, 673, 754, 842, 851, 876, 884, 886, 900, 907, 914, 919
bold, 809, 815, 817, 825, 832 851, 899, 920
limited, 501, 569, 575, 679, 827
muted, 499, 641, 642, 649, 668, 673, 676, 679
white-on-white, 569, 654
Color wheel, 397
Columns, 128, 194, 340, 630
Comfortable havens, 692–747
bathrooms, 734–735
bedrooms, 726–733
characteristics of, 694
dining rooms & breakfast nooks, 706–710
gardens, 742–747
kitchens and pantries, 711–722
libraries, dens, and offices, 723–725
living spaces, 695–706
outdoor rooms and sun rooms, 736–741
Computers and computer networks, 773, 843
Contrast, 141, 144–145
Corbels, 457
Corian, 226
Cornices, 340
Couches, 542, 626, 638, 695, 761, 864, 876
See also Settees.
Counters, 714
bluestone, 715
granite, 903
marble, 531, 662, 681, 901
quartz, 903
stainless steel, 528, 714, 768, 836
Countertops, 84–85, 104, 155, 226, 232–233
Courtyards, 294, 629, 788
Coverlets, 181, 189, 239, 261, 332, 336–337
Cupboards. *See* Armoires.
Cupboards, kitchen. *See* Cabinets, kitchen.
Curtain rods, 41, 114
Curtains, 39, 41, 44, 47–49, 55–56, 109, 111, 114–117, 178, 181, 183, 186, 191, 193, 255, 260, 264, 267, 293, 328–329, 331, 362–363, 393–394, 397, 409, 456–458, 484, 538, 555, 560, 584, 635, 771, 863, 913, 918
Cushions. *See* Pillows and cushions.

D

Decks, 135, 782, 788, 860
Decoupage, 419
Dens and offices, 38, 157, 313, 603, 608, 666, 718, 724, 771, 843, 844, 906, 908, 913
for teenagers, 911
Desks, 666, 668, 773, 923
Details, 298–355
Dining rooms, 20–21, 36, 57, 59, 100–103, 114, 150–153, 170–171, 204–207, 224–225, 242–244, 246–247, 262–265, 288–289, 306–307, 331, 345–346, 366, 371–373, 391, 396–398, 436, 473, 516 519–524, 590–597, 651–658, 706, 709, 710, 765, 827, 829–831, 891, 897, 898
Dinners, black-tie, 527
Dishes, 61–62, 280–284, 302, 418, 469, 476
Display cases, 198
Displays, 274, 286, 350
artworks, 607, 637, 646, 730, 825, 883
collections, 514, 601, 604, 614, 622, 688, 715, 717, 719, 728, 735, 757, 772, 810, 883, 894, 905, 906
decorative, 153, 157, 166, 200, 254, 274, 277, 280–284, 287, 302, 341, 418, 465, 469, 476
natural, 122, 204, 468, 478
See also Floral displays.
Docks, 741
Doors, 27, 196, 301, 340, 370, 391, 452, 680, 788, 796
glass-paned, 880
mirrored, 558
padded, 542
re-use of, 576, 592
Draperies. *See* Curtains.
Dressers, 615, 729
Dressing rooms, 541, 544
Dust mites, 777
Duvets. *See* Coverlets.

E

Eclectic environments, 572–631
- bathrooms, 621–624
- bedrooms, 610–620
- characteristics of, 574
- dining rooms and breakfast nooks, 590–597
- gardens, 629–631
- kitchens and pantries, 598–602
- libraries, dens, and offices, 603–609
- living spaces, 575–589
- outdoors rooms and sunrooms, 625–628

Elegance, 224
Engravings. *See* Prints.
Entertainment centers, 724
Entrance halls, 496, 500, 502, 504, 507, 509, 511, 583, 588, 604, 644, 809, 873, 884
Entryways, 34–35, 50–51, 75–76, 95, 194, 259, 340
Epoxy floor coating, 234
Étagères, 51

F

Fabrics, 424, 539, 641, 642, 670, 688, 771, 853, 876, 888, 897, 921
- damask, 521
- linen, 641, 652, 675, 726, 765, 812
- moleskin, 817
- remnants, 269
- tactile, 386–387, 407
- tartan, 560
- toile, 521, 549, 555, 913, 923
- vintage, 332, 343
- white, 635, 646

Faucets, 352, 532
Felt, 328
Finger bowls, 787
Fire pits, 805
Fireplaces, 32, 37, 120, 124, 148, 199, 344, 528, 535, 540, 626, 649, 670, 685, 686, 701, 754, 758, 784, 819, 827, 864, 908, 913, 934
- screens, 843

Flags, 477
Flea markets, 277
Floor coverings, 652, 698
See also Carpets.
Floor plans, open, 362–363, 409, 456
Floors, 22–24, 26, 37, 143, 152, 225, 229, 235, 394, 440, 767, 772, 836, 900
- checkerboard, 530, 851
- painted, 502, 583, 728, 888
- stone, 556, 558, 658, 751, 754, 770, 779
- waxing of, 225
- white, 888

Floral arrangements, 497, 516, 525, 560, 893, 926, 928
Floral displays, 51, 57–58, 67, 126, 161, 194–195, 275, 417, 419
Flowers and plants, 71, 137, 214–216, 296–297, 355, 426, 430, 479, 568, 753, 758, 787, 795, 803, 928
See also Plants.
Flynn, Robert, 815
Folk art, 883
Forts, 942
Fountains, 518, 563, 566
Frames, miniature, 527
Friezes, 353, 628
Fringe, 110–111, 192, 339, 511, 538
Function, 218–297
Furnishings
- aging of, 247
- arrangements, 93
- children's, 221
- pairings, 29, 30, 38, 53
- mixing styles, 28, 34, 40, 56, 76, 244, 374

Furniture, 705
- amount of, 494, 644
- antique, 578, 580, 646
- Asian, 887
- contemporary, 582, 653, 779, 821, 848
- mid-20th century, 579, 582, 823, 828
- mixed cultural, 575, 578
- mixed styles, 501, 504, 521, 575, 576, 603, 658, 665, 710, 829
- patio, 739
- wicker, 696

G

Garages, 235
Garden furniture, 245, 354, 429, 483, 489
Gardens, 68, 137, 217, 295, 296–297, 355, 431, 563–571, 629–631, 689–691, 742–747, 790–805, 866–869, 941–947
- borders, 691, 795
- formal, 569, 571, 795, 940
- labyrinth, 630
- multi-level, 568, 805
- paths, 742, 746, 795, 796, 946
- style of, 946
- walls, 796

Gazebos. 628, 790
See also Pergolas.
Glamour, 78–79, 411
Glass, 90, 413
Glassware, 81
Grapes, wine, 566
Grasses, 795
Grills, 290
Grout, 751
Guest rooms, 549, 555, 610, 612, 614, 615, 679, 726, 728, 731, 774, 776, 847, 848, 915, 918, 919, 920, 921, 926

H

Hallways, 87, 236, 251, 367
Headboards, 548, 549, 675, 846, 848, 853, 854, 914, 918, 920, 925
Heating systems, 719
Hedges, 689, 866
Herbs, 867
Hoods, cooking, 528, 664
Hooks, 235
Hutches, 37, 514, 600

I

Impact, 138–217
Islands, kitchen, 82, 226, 308–309
Ivy, 427

J

Jars, 515, 580, 802
Jars, ginger, 206, 366
Juxtapositions, 14, 261, 271, 384, 390, 395–396, 409, 442

K

Kandinsky, Wassily, 403
Kitchens, 22–25, 36, 63, 81–86, 129–131, 154, 172–173, 226–230, 248–249, 266–267, 279, 290, 308–310, 349, 374–375, 420–421, 437–438, 474–476, 528–530, 598–602, 656, 659–664, 711–722, 766–770, 833–841, 900–905
- islands, 600, 662, 717, 721, 768, 835, 837, 839, 901, 902, 903

Kusama, Yayoi, 587

L

Lamps and lighting fixtures, 535, 590, 592, 595, 602, 603, 616, 638, 650, 710, 713, 747, 771, 813, 832, 839, 851, 901, 906, 917, 927, 936
See also Light fixtures.
Landscaping, 68–71, 136–137, 792, 801

Lanterns, 788
Laptops, 773
Lattice-work, 150, 316, 867
Laundry rooms, 377
Lavender, 691, 867
Lawns, 562, 564, 691, 942
Layering, 46, 109, 334, 338, 341, 411, 450
Le Corbusier, 300
Leaf, 443
Leather, 312, 334
Libraries, 174, 234, 312, 533, 534, 535, 537, 538, 539, 540, 605, 606, 665, 723, 907, 911
Lichtenstein, Roy, 597
Light, 120, 165, 303, 341, 428
Light fixtures, 63, 79, 130, 164, 199,234, 278–279, 288, 303, 352, 473
See also Chandeliers.
Light switches, 734
Lighting systems, 830
Liquor cabinets, 445
Living rooms, 15–17, 28–33, 38, 40–44, 52–55, 77–80, 92, 96–98, 105–114, 147, 167, 178–184, 195–198, 202–203, 222–223, 237–242, 304, 317–323, 328, 361- 365, 370, 384–389, 393–395, 412–416, 444, 465–466, 470–471, 494, 499, 501, 505, 507, 508, 511, 513, 575–588, 635–643, 645–650, 695–699, 703–705, 751, 754, 757–761, 810–822, 875, 883, 885
Lockers, 235, 737
Loggias, 625, 786
Logs, 120, 122
Lucite, 103, 401

M

Majolica, 282
Mantels, 56, 58, 110, 275, 468, 506, 645, 667, 757, 758
Maps, 127, 439, 470, 637
Maquettes, 499
Marbleizing, 394
Marquetry, faux, 502
Masks, 607, 843
Materials, re-use of, 801
Media rooms, 80
Microwaves, 663
Millwork, 87, 349
Minimalism, 644
Mirrors, 16–17, 34–35, 57, 64, 78–79, 124–125, 131, 162, 184, 194, 198, 210–211, 275, 285, 372, 441, 452, 471, 506, 513, 534, 580, 615, 616, 621, 623, 670, 765, 816, 847, 922
Molding, 16–17, 314
Monograms, 542
Moses, Ed, 821
Mudrooms, 235
Murals, 305, 353, 523, 588, 833

N

Nails, decorative, 306, 312, 318, 321,322, 388
Napkins, 944
Natural abodes, 748–805
bathrooms, 780–781
bedrooms, 774–779
characteristics of, 750
dining rooms and breakfast nooks, 762–765
gardens, 790–805
kitchens and pantries, 766–770
libraries, dens, and offices, 771–773
living spaces, 751–761
outdoor rooms and sun rooms, 782–789
Nelson, George, 602

O

Offices, home, 87, 227, 311, 368, 449 *See also* Dens and offices.
Onyx, 556
Ostrich eggs, 595
Ottomans, 252, 511, 626, 641, 676,700, 773, 875, 908
Outdoor rooms & sunrooms, 559–561, 625–628, 685–688, 736–741, 782–789, 859–865, 930–940
Ovens, 721

P

Paint, 359, 378, 380, 440, 446, 454, 486, 489, 776
chalkboard, 221
peeling, 304, 305, 454
Paintings, 496
floral, 816, 926, 928
modern, 587, 595, 607, 809, 815, 821
Paisley, 192
Palette. *See* Color.
Paneling, 15, 18, 142, 222–223, 229, 312, 316, 437, 441
Pantries, 81, 531, 662
Parlors, 19, 240
Parterres, 562, 563
Parties, 347, 421
Parzinger, Tommi, 823
Patios and terraces, 133, 214–215, 289, 292, 294–295, 480, 484
See also Terraces.
Patterns, 40–43, 44, 46–48, 54, 116, 142, 143–146, 152–153, 160, 164–165,169, 175, 179, 182–183, 192, 204, 246, 255, 270, 319, 323, 329, 331, 337, 388, 397–398, 404, 411, 422, 425, 494, 502, 553, 580, 642, 670, 844, 853
check, 883, 891
floral, 515, 560, 854
geometric, 579, 583, 931
gingham, 888
striped, 822, 844, 848, 913
Pavilions, 685, 686, 747, 784
Pelmets, 327
Pergolas, 290, 353, 798
Photographs, 578, 646, 825
See also Artwork.
Picnics, 944
Pictures. *See* Artwork.
Pietra Cardosa, 232
Pillows, 116, 125, 179–180, 184, 251, 261–262, 266, 269, 272, 291, 314, 330, 342, 351 400–401, 407, 410, 425, 460, 480, 487, 502, 505, 542, 580, 605, 654, 688, 697, 703, 736, 805, 817, 830, 875, 876, 897, 908, 911, 914, 925, 932
Pinecones, 123
Piping, 43, 318, 324, 390
Pitchers, 276, 905
Place cards, 527
Place settings, 347–348
Plaids, 338, 351, 396
Planters, 294, 426, 474, 483, 485, 837
Plants, 559, 560, 566, 569, 571, 745, 747, 753, 765, 786, 795, 798, 803, 867, 941, 946
See also Flowers and plants.
Plate racks, 719
Playrooms, 221
Plumbing, 734
Polyurethane, 225
Ponds, 214–215
Pool houses and rooms, 134, 212, 258, 291, 626, 859, 860
Pools, 67, 70, 132, 136, 213, 685, 860, 868, 940
Porcelain, 514
Porches, 98, 353, 423, 478, 481, 486–487, 560, 688, 736, 863, 932, 934, 936
Pottery, 468
Portraits, 506
Posters, 848, 873
Pots, kitchen, 840

Pottery, 757
Prints, 516, 533, 537, 597
See also Artwork.
Proportion, 471

Q
Quick fixes, 432–489
Quilts, 181, 379
Quince, 926

R
Railings, 18
Rain sensors, 819
Rattan, 238, 250, 254, 424
Reading areas, 93, 174, 234, 400, 605, 650, 723, 880, 917
Refrigerators, wine, 663
Remote controls, 815
Ribbon, 445
Rocks, 768
Roman Notes (painting), 204
Rooms
large, 493, 494, 501, 584, 638, 695, 876, 889
small, 704, 705, 888
Rosemary, 867
Rugs. *See* Carpets.

S
Saarinen, Eero, 829
Scale, 42, 43, 394
Sconces, 366, 441
Screens, 500, 659
folded, 88, 197, 311, 452, 541
Sculptures, 689
Seat cushions, 448
Seating areas, 30, 180, 248, 289, 293
Serene retreats, 632–691
bathrooms, 681–684
bedrooms, 668–680
characteristics of, 634
dining rooms and breakfast nooks, 651–658
gardens, 689–691
kitchens and pantries, 659–664
libraries, dens, and offices, 665–667
living spaces, 635–650
outdoor rooms and sun rooms, 685–688
Settees, 687
Louis XV, 505
Louis XVI, 502
Regency, 500
See also Sofas.
Shade (color), 407, 422
Shades. *See* Window treatments.
Shadows, 120
Shells, 122, 468
Shelves, 38, 62, 81, 86–87, 151, 154, 230, 234, 254, 257, 281, 371, 444, 449, 469, 477, 714, 715, 717, 731, 766, 770, 899
Shower curtains, 463, 929
Showers
bathroom, 91, 165
outdoor, 133, 482
Shutters, 427, 455, 680, 686
Simplicity, 72–137
Sinks, 937
bathroom, 680, 781, 856
kitchen, 308, 662
Sitting rooms. *See* Parlors.
Sky, 428
Skylights, 819
Slipcovers, 261, 263, 319, 521, 591, 635, 646, 765, 827, 891
Sofas, 32–33, 38, 44, 97, 102–103, 122, 168, 177, 236–237, 241, 251, 253, 317–319, 384, 444, 471
legs, 317
See also Couches.
Space, 42, 46, 56, 141, 159, 230
Sophisticated surroundings, 490–571
bathrooms, 556–558
bedrooms, 541–555
characteristics of, 492
dining rooms and breakfast nooks, 514–527
gardens, 562–571
kitchens and pantries, 528–532
libraries, dens, and offices, 533–540
living spaces, 493–513
outdoor rooms and sun rooms, 559–561
Sound systems, 836
Spaces, separation of, 592, 659, 767, 880, 905
Sponges, sea, 478
Stair rails, 810
Staircases and stairwells, 75, 644, 783, 810, 876
Stairs, 360
Statues, 534, 576, 667, 854
Stencils, 511
Steps, 68–69
Stone, 136, 164, 213, 232, 499, 556
Stone walls, 564
Stools, 30, 286, 421, 445, 580, 588, 596, 625, 896
bar, 602, 656, 664, 837, 839
Storage, 257, 400, 623, 719, 722, 729, 878
Stoves, wood, 939
Strié, 378
Stripes, 165, 175, 272, 338, 397
Studies. *See* Dens.
Styles
bold, 806–869
comfortable, 692–747
eclectic, 572–631
natural, 748–805
serene, 632–691
sophisticated, 490–571
welcoming, 870–947
Suede, 386–387, 390
Sunlight, 538, 661, 758
Sunrooms, 27, 66, 98, 286, 316, 339, 408–409, 443
Suzanis, 609, 619
Swings, 486–487, 942
Symmetry, 14, 18, 53, 344
porch, 736, 934

T
Table settings, 61
Tablecloths, 51, 259, 348, 459, 463, 519, 739, 827, 929
Tables, 51, 95, 104, 245, 527, 584, 604, 613, 651, 658, 665, 688, 706, 707, 709, 710, 762, 781, 824, 829, 835, 864, 889, 895, 939
bistro, 656
coffee, 237, 238, 317, 401, 471, 511, 603, 815, 863, 864
console, 34–35, 53
dining room, 36–37, 170–171, 207, 240, 243–244, 247, 278, 370–371, 446
end, 237, 251, 603, 703, 917
kitchen, 172–173, 309
night, 253, 285
Parsons, 710
Regency, 523
rectory, 595
round, 243, 249, 493, 523, 524, 527, 596, 656, 844
Tableware and china, 519, 601
Tapestries, 592
See also Wall hangings.
Tassels, 312, 348
Teak, 292, 354, 483, 489
Teapots, 281, 905
Televisions, 704, 718, 843
Television cabinets, 325, 451
Tents, 425
Terraces, 860, 864, 867, 868, 933, 940 *See also* Patios and terraces.

Textures, 18, 22, 47, 76, 113, 114, 146, 160, 311, 334, 642
Throws. *See* Coverlets.
Tiles
- bathroom, 90–91, 383
- fireplace, 148, 344
- floor, 22, 26, 37, 90, 152, 598, 735, 751
- kitchen, 267, 309–310, 349, 376
- wall, 622, 681, 711, 768, 827, 841, 857, 858

Toile, 48, 270, 335, 382, 406, 450
Topiaries, 583
Towels, 780, 781
- dish, 944

Trays, 894
Trees, 630, 691, 768, 868, 942
Trim, 43, 44, 185, 186, 293, 318, 324, 326, 328, 339, 388
Trim, decorative, 584, 847
Trompe l'oeil, 833
Troughs, re-use of, 937
Tubs, bathroom, 26, 64, 91
Twombly, Cy, 204

U

Upholstery, 100, 105–106, 121, 174, 178, 236, 238, 246, 251, 292, 384, 386–387, 424, 444, 502, 505, 518, 521, 539, 584, 587, 595, 638, 846
- leather, 521, 523, 610, 654, 706, 824, 876
- white, 635, 824

Urns, 516, 525, 571, 765

V

Vanities, 462, 683, 856, 858
Vases, 275, 341, 410, 417, 473, 497, 606, 645, 829
Venetian plaster, 76, 148
Vertical files, 254
Views, 55, 94, 101, 260, 296, 651, 666, 684, 689, 741, 754, 766, 771, 773, 774, 784, 802, 860
Vines, 485

W

Wainscoting, 149, 151, 373, 442
Wall coverings, fabric, 48, 188, 333
Wall hangings, 42, 189, 200, 306, 332, 342, 545, 590, 592, 609, 884
Wallpaper, 151, 156, 158–159, 161, 163, 200, 314, 353, 366–368, 381–382, 450, 511, 706, 735, 816, 899
- Chinese, 525
- hand-painted, 494, 506, 512, 515

Walls, 76, 96, 141, 147, 152, 188, 200, 305–307, 311–316, 333, 337, 359, 361, 364, 369, 372, 374, 384, 393, 395, 423, 435, 439, 538, 548, 583, 596, 711, 772, 780, 825, 888, 900, 914, 921
- bamboo-covered, 754
- blue, 919
- color of, 642, 661, 900, 902, 919
- glass, 761, 765
- glazed, 506
- grass cloth covered, 777
- green, 642, 661
- lacquered, 523, 578
- mirrored, 558, 675
- paneled, 579, 624, 810, 825, 844, 876, 899
- partial, 880
- upholstered, 605
- white, 578, 624, 654, 701, 825, 899
- yellow, 900, 902

Wardrobes, 544
Water features, 563, 566, 631, 651
Welcoming homes, 870–947
- bathrooms, 927–929
- bedrooms, 914–926
- characteristics of, 872
- dining rooms and breakfast nooks, 889–899
- gardens, 941–947
- kitchens and pantries, 900–905
- libraries, dens, and offices, 906–913
- living spaces, 873–888
- outdoor rooms and sun rooms, 930–940

Wicker, 455
Window seats, 257, 266, 268, 458, 650, 851, 875, 878, 880, 903
Window treatments, 48, 60, 80, 107, 114, 118, 185–186, 262, 266, 272, 326–327, 537, 538, 560, 584, 609, 664, 676, 726, 780, 907, 930
- *See also* Curtains.

Windows, 181, 185–186, 237, 340, 384, 754, 770, 780, 784, 819, 848
Wisteria, 747, 786, 867
Wood and woodwork, 34, 36, 225, 311, 499, 509, 523, 624, 681, 767, 768, 779
Wreaths, 464